Dedication

To Tina,
my lovely wife and my friend,
for loving and believing in me with all your heart.

To Karly and Aria
the fruit of my labor, for being born.

To the Living Water,
for bringing forth new life and quenching my thirst.

I love you all!

Out of the Desert Flow Rivers
Copyright © 2017, 2018 by Joel Kibble.

All rights reserved. No part of this book may be used or reproduced in any manner whatsoever without prior written permission of the author/publisher; except in the case of brief quotations embodied in reviews.

ePub Edition April 2017
This title is also available in audiobook.
www.joelkibble.com

Scripture quotations are from
The Hebrew-Greek Key Word Study Bible
King James Version
Second Revised Edition
Copyright 1984, 1990, 2008, by AMG International, Inc.
All Rights Reserved

Airman's Pocket Bible
Copyright 2004 by Holman Bible Publishers
Nashville, TN. All Rights Reserved

Holman Christian Standard Bible
Copyright 1999, 2000, 2002, 2003
By Holman Bible Publishers

Interior and Cover Design: Watersprings Media House

Healing Rivers Publishing
P.O. Box 33, Brentwood, TN 37024
1-800-480-9057

ISBN 978-0-9846743-1-2

OUT OF THE DESERT FLOW RIVERS

By

Joel Kibble

Contents

Preface	6
Acknowledgements	9
Introduction	10
BREAKING THE CYCLE	**11**
Going Through the Motions	12
Rest	15
Walking as He Walked	19
Worry	22
Sowing	25
Who Goes Before You?	28
Old Man, New Man	31
Gossip	34
HEALING	**37**
Forgiveness	38
Confession	42
Freedom	46
Turning Up the Heat	49
Color of Character	52
RESTORATION	**55**
Death	56
Self-Worth	58

Purpose	60
The Blessing of Job	63
Little Lad's Lunch	66
What Doest Thou Here?	69
Let Me Fix It	72
Fire!	74
EMPOWERMENT	*79*
David	80
Courage	84
Focus	87
Vision	90
Temptation	93
Called and Chosen	95
Consider	97
Victory	100
To Shine by Night	102
It Needs More Salt!	104
Truth	107
Diamond	110
Don't Become Weary	113
Answering with Faith	116
About the Author	119

Preface

"Out of the Desert Flow Rivers"

Just because you grow up Christian doesn't mean you KNOW God! You would think that by being a pastor's kid, by hearing the Bible read every day, by attending Christian schools for all of the 16 years of my educational stint so far, that I'd have a four-star relationship with God---you would THINK! Not. Even as an adult, as a member of the 10-time Grammy Award-winning group, Take 6, with over 20 years singing about God as my job, 10 years speaking about God and close to 10 years writing about my experiences with God would I have it down pat. Instead, as most individuals, I've suffered more than a few setbacks and disappointments. My desert experiences throughout my life have led me to seek the flowing river of healing that comes from daily, persistently, seeking to KNOW God.

Somewhere in my developmental stages, I'd learned that when you do what's right, say what's right, and as far as possible, BE right, you are repaid with blessings. So, when my parents' divorce devastated our family, and my divorce devastated me again with my own family, I began to feel the guilt and despair of having failed of being right. I've suffered addictions to various vices, and sustained deep psychological wounds from broken, dysfunctional relationships and low self-esteem. I became angry with the idea that I'd lived this Christian lifestyle but was powerless to keep bad things from happening, and seemingly unable to get God's attention. It was during this period of my life, when root issues reared their ugly heads and I dangled on the edge of a mental meltdown, that I found myself calling out to this invisible and seemingly inaudible God. Looking for God to answer was like languishing in an arid desert, panting for water. Apparently, I didn't know Him as well as I thought. "If You exist," I snarled with clenched teeth, "and if You have any interest in me at all, I'm calling You out to show Yourself. Speak to me like You spoke to all these ancient biblical characters I've read about! Show Yourself as real or let me live my own life the way I want!"

God's got many different ways of communicating with each member of His creation. I've found that He can speak audibly or inaudibly, through His written word or by His spoken word, by another human being, like His prophet Elijah or by a creature such as Balaam's donkey, through circumstances or experiences, through nature, through processes, through dreams, through songs, etc. His ability to speak is at least as varied as the different types of personalities on this earth. And any way that He chooses is one in which I would uniquely understand in the way I would best receive it at the moment.

I honestly don't remember the way God answered me on that day that I challenged myself to be real with Him. What I do remember is that from then on, He began to pull the cotton from my ears and the scales from my eyes by making me aware of all His ways of communication that I had been blinded to.

Out of the Desert Flow Rivers, is a collection of blogs originally written for Take 6's website. I decided to share the revelations and lessons that I learned with others who might have been confused, frustrated, burned out, or simply didn't know how to recognized the voice of the Creator. I don't believe everyone needs to make the same mistakes that I have, and if I've gained some insights into God's character, why not pass them on to others? I also believe that the principles upon which lessons are based are universal, but the applications to the principles are unique to each individual. So, as you read, pray that God shows you the principle involved, then ask that He show you how each one applies to your own life.

Acknowledgements

To the many supporters and fans of Take 6 who kept the demand going for "Rivers" blogs, and who encouraged with their supportive comments, I express a gracious "thank-you!"

To the members of Take 6, past and present, I thank you and your encouragement and contribution to this work. Without the support of family and friends, who challenged me, sharpened me and gave me vital feedback, this work could not have been honed.

Special thanks goes to Ms. LaRhonda McKnight and Dr. Nicolette Rose for your passion for the English language and your dedication of your time and effort.

I also thank April Rushing for your support and organizational skill, and Elder Steven Norman for challenging me to reach out with the hand of faith to get this project finished, and for your patience while I contemplated the task.

To Elder T. Marshall Kelly, for your continual prayers on my behalf, to Eric Thomas and Associates for the seed that set this project in motion, and to Hallerin Hill for your creative approaches to excellence, Thank You.

To all the brothers and sisters who make up my inner circle of spiritual support and accountability, my victories are your victories as well!

Introduction

I've learned that my passion is based upon the ministry of reconciling others to their loving Maker. The four key areas include: Breaking Negative Cycles, Healing, Restoration and Empowerment. The entries I have included in the book fall into one of these previously mentioned categories.

There are three different ways that you may approach the lessons in this book. You may, (1) read from the beginning to the end, an entry a day, or you may (2) pray that God leads you to an entry that applies to you at the moment as you thumb through the titles of the entries, or (3) read entries by categories, according to what subject you feel is most pertinent.

It is my desire that you, the reader, will find that God is near and reachable, He is most interested in your well-being, and He actually wants you to live an abundant life that is full of joy. I pray that your ears might be opened to the many ways He calls you. I pray that His refreshing word will rush forth out of the midst of your desert experience, like rivers.

BREAKING THE CYCLE

Going Through the Motions

"And let us not be weary in well doing: for in due season we shall reap, if we faint not." Galatians 6:9

Most of the people who have known me for a long time have known that I have always been a swimmer. Between the ages of 7 and 14, I swam for various swim teams in Alabama; finally joining a Junior Olympic team in Huntsville.

The swimming schedule was hectic. Every afternoon during the school year, I would leave school at 3 p.m. and head directly to swimming practice for two to two and a half hours. The remainder of the evening would be devoted to doing homework until bedtime. Twice a week, I would be required to attend early morning training before school for an hour and a half, rising at 4:30 a.m. to be on time. When school ended for the summer break, most of the kids departed for vacation fun, but training for me was increased to every morning and every afternoon. Needless-to-say, it seemed as though there was not enough time in the day to do what I wanted to do before returning to the swimming pool.

In practice, most of the workout was devoted to technique and muscle training, spending large amounts of time exploding from the starting blocks and speeding up the flip turns at the other end. I cannot forget to mention the drudgery of long distance swimming, and the lung-burning sprints. We were required to swim with floats positioned between our legs, while our feet were bound together to strengthen our arms. Then we kicked for miles holding on to a kickboard to strengthen our legs. Day in and day out, summer after school year, school year after summer, this was my schedule.

It is an understatement to say that I was bored to tears at times. The possibility of hanging out with friends and getting to know girls often gave way to that perpetual black line at the bottom of the pool. I hated the fact that I did not have much of a social life, and while my body was in training, my mind was often somewhere else. Many times, I felt that my heart was not in it. I was just going through the motions, and because of that, I felt like I was simply "faking it." I often questioned myself. "If my heart is not into the grueling swimming practices," I thought, "shouldn't I just quit and find something else that excites me? Why should I continue to go through the motions?" "I'm not accomplishing anything!"

Well, going through the motions does accomplish something. The truth of the matter is that all the instances of "going through the motions," whether my heart was in it or not, taught my muscles proper muscle response that only consistency could do. Long afternoons of endless distance stroking, which I could have accomplished in my sleep, exemplify how much was spent repeating the same motions. However, those motions were being committed to muscle memory every morning before school and every afternoon following school. When the big swimming competitions came, I simply needed to allow my body to do what it had been trained to do for years. I could then focus on doing my best rather than focusing on executing technique. Proper technique had been firmly entrenched into my soul during the drudgery of the many hours of practice I had logged over the years.

Interestingly enough, I owe the blue ribbons, trophies, and victories to the process of "going through the motions." It's funny then, that I have since decided that, in life, going through the motions has been less than noble. The process of going through the right motions is not fruitless, no matter how monotonous.

There have been a thousand times since that I've found myself going through the motions with marriage, child rearing, Take 6, ministry, family duties, finances, health issues, interpersonal relationships, etc. I can truly say that my heart has been in and out of each of these commitments. Perhaps the reason God admonishes us not to "be weary in well-doing" is because quite often, we may not be "feeling it." At times, "doing well" may feel like nothing more than going through the motions, but the right motions do accomplish something.

If you feel that you are going through the motions in some aspect of your life, take courage — "feeling it" is not a requirement in doing God's will — but trusting Him does play its part. Your heart will return if you "faint not." No matter what you are feeling or not feeling, with God, you will find that while *going* through the motions, you have been *growing* through the motions...right into what He wants you to be.

Rest

"Let us labor therefore to enter into that rest, lest any man fall after the same example of unbelief." Hebrews 4:11

There are quite a few definitions for the word "rest." Some of them include a state or period of refreshing freedom from exertion, or the cessation of movement or action. In terms of a particular thought that I would like to share with you, I will focus on the entry that defines rest as freedom from mental or emotional anxiety.

A few weeks into the Fall season, I finally turned on the heat to our house as the days began to turn cold. But I was perplexed to learn that every time the house reached the desired temperature, the gas pilot to the furnace would go out, resulting in cold air blowing through the vents. I would descend into the basement to manually light the pilot to the old furnace only to have it shut off again.

I finally decided to bite the bullet and call AC and Heating service to come take a look, hoping that the problem was a simple, dirty valve to be cleaned, but to my dismay, the problem turned out to be much worse. The technician found that the heating exchange in our furnace had three holes and a crack in it, clearly exposing us to carbon monoxide fumes, the danger of the unit catching fire, or both. The unit was condemned, and the gas to it was shut off, leaving the house without central heat. After 21 years of service, the unit had seen its last days. I'd anticipated aging appliances when I signed up for home insurance a few years ago, but unfortunately the company I chose was notorious for finding a thousand reasons not to honor claims. With predictions of record low temperatures looming in the coming winter, and the cost of a new furnace in the upwards of $7000 to $15,000 more than we had, to say that I got "anxious" was an understatement.

I decided that I had to break to the news to my wife Tina, and my daughter, Karly. Just recently married, I felt bad informing her that the unit had failed, almost as though my ability to provide for my family had also failed, but with a short response of faith, Tina reminded me that God had provided for my air conditioning unit to be fixed a couple of summers ago, and that He would also provide for this urgency, despite the fact that we only had about $1500 in the bank. We made a list of God's promises to us, and a list of recent answers to prayer and thanked God for having already answered our need, though I had no idea what would happen.

But I was definitely encouraged a bit as I solemnly informed my daughter after picking her up from school. Her three innocent questions seemed to suddenly put everything into perspective. "Are we going to freeze to death?" "No, silly!" I responded. "We won't freeze." "Will we have to wear heavy clothes to bed?" She inquired. "Of course not!" I laughed. "Will we have to sleep in the same bed together to keep warm?" she asked. "Oh no," I said, chuckling at her extreme mental preparations. Without another word Karly resumed her quiet activity, leaving me wondering who of the two of us had more faith. She was so convinced that the issue would be handled that she hardly broke focus on the craft she was working on to even look at me while challenging my faith. In fact, both Tina and Karly so trusted that we were going to be okay that they came to a point of mental rest. They resumed their normally scheduled activities; for had this been a real emergency, I would have been notified by the looks on their faces.

The writer of the book of Hebrews speaks of such a rest in chapter 4:1-11. He warns us in verse 1 not to "come short" of entering into the rest that God has for us today. As an example, the author uses the experience of the children of Israel in the desert to explain what "entering into God's rest meant." The children of Israel were involved in a heated situation, waiting for God to lead them through the desert, into the Canaan land. This land was the result of a promise God had made to His children. He promised that He would personally lead them from Egypt to Canaan, a land that was as rich and sweet as milk and honey.

There was one key condition, though; Israel had to believe that what God said was what He would accomplish. Believing should have been simple ... right? Surprisingly, that was hard to do.

There is a sense of rest that occurs when we hear God's promises, and then choose to believe them to be true. Think about it...if we believe that what God is promising us is anything less than true, then we have to look out for ourselves and cover our backs, right? Maybe the conditions around us have changed since God made His promise to us. Maybe the pressures around us have intensified and the heat is becoming unbearable. Maybe God found something else to do in the meantime and forgot how long we have been waiting. The truth is, you will either let God cover your back, or you will try to cover it yourself, but the moment we stop believing that He will look out for us is the moment we enter the state of unrest and anxiety. This is the "coming short" that Paul warned about in Hebrews 4:1. "For we which have believed do enter into rest..." Hebrews 4:3.

Observe the state of the world right now and note the widespread unrest. Why is there such angst? God said that we would witness end-time catastrophic events taking place, and He encouraged us to see these events as signs that His coming was near; yet, the anxiety level of the world remains high. With such a message of hope, why are we still anxious? "...And they to whom it was first preached entered not in (to rest) because of unbelief," Hebrews 4:6. If we believe God's promise, our belief should result in a sense of inner peace.

Two days later, by the way, my AC/Heating technician was knocking at the back door, waiting to install a brand-new furnace. Unfortunately, my original unit's brand was out of stock, so I had to be upgraded to more efficient unit. Don't you hate when that happens? Of course, as a punch line that only God can orchestrate, how much do you supposed it all cost me? $1495.00. Brand new, more efficient unit, automated thermostat...saved $5.00. Awe of my Father? Priceless.

Here is the sum. You must know what God's promises are to you. You must then believe Him. If you know His promises and believe Him, then you will rest in His Word to you. So, take inventory of your thoughts. In what areas are you living in a state of unrest? What are you anxious about? What did God say about addressing anxiety? What needs to be done?

Hear the Promise: Philippians 4:6, 7

Walking as He Walked

"He that saith he abideth in Him ought himself also so to walk, even as He walked." I John 2:6

When I first heard about the new hurricane named Katrina moving across the tip of Florida, I was unimpressed. As you know, I am a frustrated storm chaser. Whenever I watch nature programs about the destructive power of weather systems, I am inundated with the scenes on the screen. While I was excited about this exceptional hurricane season, Katrina seemed as though its weakened power would not even register on the scoreboard; but Katrina's target was not Florida.

Katrina tiptoed over into the Gulf of Mexico, and there it received the power and authority to accomplish its mission. Its eye was focused on the Gulf States. There in warmed water, Katrina worked herself up into a massive, angry rage. Like one of those little spinning tops that I used to play with as a child, when she was wound up into a wild frenzy she marches off with the energy of half a million nuclear bombs set to trample the cities in her path.

I was not really surprised by the high gale-force winds or the floods that came afterward as much as I was floored by what I saw after the storm had passed. I was transfixed on what the waters of Katrina brought to the surface. The presence and lack of compassion that demonstrated itself in the next couple of days was astounding to me. There is one thing that I have learned about adversity; it will bring to the surface the core of what a person really thinks. If there is little compassion in one's soul, adversity will bring it out. If someone truly thinks he is better than other people are, harsh conditions will bring it out. If there is a genuine love for people, hardship will bring it out. If there exists a true pity for suffering in the heart, extreme circumstances will reveal it.

Think of the many nameless heroes who stayed behind at their own risk to care for those who could not leave, or the many who drove all the way down to the city limits loaded down with rescue supplies only to be turned away. Many a maintenance worker chose not to leave the apartment complex they worked for, accepting rather to suffer with tenants who had no help, than save themselves. Many doctors and nurses chose not to punch out after their shift and chose to keep the patients comfortable with the medical supplies on hand, rather than be transported to safety. One musician chose to head directly to the convention center, the heart of the awful confusion, just to lend his influence in keeping people encouraged, and to bring attention to the lack of relief. Through adversity, the true nature of Christ was demonstrated in the face of blatant unconcern.

Christians have read in God's Word that as the end of time approaches, these types of events would take place (Mark 13:3-8). I do not believe that we are supposed to stand idly by and watch as the world suffers, though. Sorry to say, but, there will be many more devastating events such as Hurricane Katrina. Even as I write and you read, there are more hurricanes forming in the mid-Atlantic. There is more injustice occurring in the streets and in the workplace. There are famines in various countries decimating thousands of people. Many people will be put out of their homes and will cry out for help. As unfortunate as these events are, they are excellent opportunities for Jesus to walk the Earth again. What do I mean? The life and character of Jesus Christ can be demonstrated in each of these disasters. While the needs of His people are being met, His Words can be spoken and His healing power felt, to prepare His people for His coming.

There is still time!

What is our mission but to demonstrate the loving character of Jesus Christ in these times? I believe it is the desire of our great enemy to have us hide in our comfort zones, our lovely houses, under our comfortable jobs, and behind our church walls while people are still reeling from misfortune.

In John 17:15, Jesus prayed not that His followers would be taken out of the world, but that they would be kept from evil while they were in the world. Verse 18 says that we have been sent into the world. Jesus also prays in verse 26 that the love that God has for Him may also be found in His followers. So how is the love of God demonstrated in these times?

When the disasters strike, we should be poised and ready to initiate rescue in any of its needed forms, even before the world takes action. We should be prepared to demonstrate the character of Jesus even as He is on His way back.

What has He called you to be for Him in this day and hour? How would Jesus have responded to the victims of Hurricane Katrina? How is His life being walked out in you? Jesus still walks the Earth today. How does your life show it?

***Go Deeper:** Galatians 6: 2, 9*

Worry

*"Therefore, don't worry about tomorrow,
because tomorrow will worry about itself.
Each day has enough trouble of its own." Matthew 6:34*

One of the worst things we can do to ourselves is to worry about tomorrow. The enemy wears our poor souls out by throwing out scenarios of the future and possible conclusions to them. They always start out from a place of concern, but they end up at the shores of discouragement and despair. We can only live one day at a time, and that is all God means for us to live.

I have seen this principle played out many times since I have been with Take 6, especially when it comes to touring. On many occasions, our management will present for profitability the scenario of tours that are months long in duration. Because I am a family man, it feels torturous for me to be away for long periods in locations that take me to the other side of the world. The enemy's line of suggested scenarios begins: "What if something goes terribly wrong while you are on the other side of the world? How will your relationship hold up when you have not been together for so long a time? Marriages fail for such reasons. How will you address the situation if a thief breaks into your home while you are gone? What if your child's heart condition flares up and she collapses while you are in the backcountry of Poland? You do realize that it took 16 hours of travel to your destination, and the airlines only have one return flight every couple of days? What if your wife is involved in an awful car accident and you cannot get back soon enough? How will you handle that?"

I feel pressured to emotionally walk out and live these scenes months before the tour even starts, accounting for circumstances that may not even happen. Has this occurred on some level to you in your experience? The enemy attempts to try to get you to live tomorrow's challenges and trials today.

While you cannot physically live but one day at a time, you can emotionally attempt to live two or more days at a time, and you can suffer for it terribly.

A friend gave me an analogy that stuck fast in my mind. He said that the human stomach produces enough acid sufficient to burn one meal at a time. We see the effects when even a small amount of stomach acid backs up into the esophagus in awful heartburn. But, what if our stomachs produced in one moment all the acid needed for the entire day? Imagine the horrid effects if it produced acid proportionate to two days, two weeks, or two months in advance of the meals we would eat.

Now picture what we do to our emotional lives by living the fears, insecurities, and worries of events months, weeks, or even days down the line. Have you stopped to think that we have no guarantees that the scenarios the enemy presents will even turn out the way he suggests, and in all this, we have then undermined and underestimated the power of God and the wonderful "plans that He has" for us," (Jeremiah 29:11).

God will give grace for one day at a time, because we can only live one day at a time. He does not give grace for tomorrow, because tomorrow has not come yet. Often, I have seen God miraculously shorten tours that I thought were too long. I have also seen Him give me grace to handle long tours, so that they passed almost without notice. Most importantly, He has handled dire emergencies with my family while I have been absolutely inaccessible while on the road, and oftentimes without my knowledge. And, by the way, what makes me think that being present at home during the time of an emergency would make the circumstances any less critical? I still have to call on God for security or comfort. God rescues our families and us anyway, while we are at home or abroad!

You can only live one day at a time, and, consequently, God chooses to disperse His grace daily. Each day has enough trouble of its own. So why do you choose to compound today's challenges with tomorrow's, which only amounts to worry? According to Matthew 6:27: "Can any of you add a single cubit to his height by worrying?" So, choose to rest in God's arms, and let Him handle the unknown. "But seek first the kingdom of God and His right-eousness, and all these things will be provided for you." (vs. 33).

Sowing

"But this I say, He which soweth sparingly shall reap also sparingly; and he which soweth bountifully, shall reap also bountifully," II Corinthians 9:6

A baby shower was being coordinated for a good friend of mine in New Jersey, so after Take 6's show in Bethesda, Maryland, I decided to hang around and visit my sister, Michelle, who also resides in Maryland. On Sunday of that weekend, I packed up the car and left for New Jersey. I decided that I would be the hidden-help guy; running all errands and doing the little knick-knack things that normally keep the honored parents-to-be in a state of panic, ultimately missing the import of the celebration. So, while everybody was preparing the house for guests, I stole away to get a gift for the parents-to-be from Babies-R-Us.

I'm a penny pincher. But I do pride myself in the fact that I always think of the "necessary items" that they will need...which, actually, happen to be the least expensive items, too; but between me and you, at the bottom of my little grinchy heart, I just didn't want to spend money. After all, I was spending money to be there for my friends. I've already contributed to the occasion ... right? Well, that was what I was thinking.

On the way to the baby store, though, I remembered the shower that was given for my daughter, Karly, before she was born. Friends from all over came to join in the celebration, and Karly was blessed with so much, that she didn't want for ANYTHING...not even diapers. Even the most expensive items on the registry were purchased. I considered not registering for the strollers and car seats, thinking to buy these items myself if I wanted them; but these items were included in the registry anyway...I mean, it could not hurt to at least register for them, right? To my dismay, EVERYTHING was purchased! I came home and had to drop to my knees to thank God for EVERYTHING. Through the seed that friends and family had sown, God had supplied Karly's needs in abundance.

Suddenly, back in New Jersey, I found myself petitioning God on the way to the baby store. "Please leave the most expensive item for me, Lord. I want to purchase it!" This was my way of sowing into the lives of these parents-to-be. I was blessed in abundance...I wanted to bless others in abundance! The few hundred dollars I had jealously sworn to save from the Japanese tour, I was supposed to put toward my $3,500 college bill. Of course, that was not nearly enough. I knew I would not graduate from college without paying that bill, but I knew it was time to sow in to someone else's life. I sacrificed what I had, forsook my grinchy, penny-pinching little heart, and spent the rest of my extra money on the stroller and car seat for my friends.

Of course, it all felt good until I got home and eyed that college bill again. What had I done?! A few seconds of inspiration on Sunday had led to a crisis and anxiety on Monday.

About two days later, I received a call from the nice woman in my college advisor's office. She was calling because she happened to be reviewing my bill in anticipation of my graduation. She asked me if I had been given any extra books for classes that I did not need. I did have extra books, but at this point, they couldn't be returned. "Oh, well, that's okay," she said. "After reviewing your bill, we were able to find quite a few duplicate charges, though. When adjustments are made, you should only owe $1,760, not $3,500."

Hmmm, let's do the math...
I spend about $300 for the stroller and car seat,

Suddenly, $1,740 is subtracted from my $3,500 college bill! Let's see here...what's the word I'm looking for... HALLELUJAH??!!

For me the world stopped spinning for just a moment, and the only presence I felt was the presence of God around me. I felt Him smiling at me the way I now smile at my daughter when she looks up at me with a new toy in her mouth. "That's the law of sowing and reaping, son," God said. It was not the dollar amount as much as the generosity of spirit.

When you sow bountifully, you reap bountifully. If you sow sparingly, as I have most of my life, you reap sparingly. Do you want a great harvest? Then sow a great crop. In fact, pray for a great amount of seed to sow a great crop. Seed does not only need to stand for money. Sow energy, time, means, words, resources, relationship, kindness, mercy, forgiveness, grace, love, etc. What kind of crop do you want? Sow that kind of seed. And, remember, if you sow one seed, you don't reap one piece of fruit. You get a few pieces of fruit with many more seeds. You can end it there, or continue to sow a great crop. That is up to you. What would you like to see happen next year? Five years? Ten years? Sow it now and sow big.

Woman at the advisor's office, your harvest is coming! Do not worry; you just keep on sowing into the lives of God's children, and thank you for being a blessing to me!

Sow More Deeply: *Proverbs 11:24, 25; Hosea 10:12; Acts 20:35; II Corinthians 9:6-11; Galatians 6:7*

Who Goes Before You?

*"Understand this day, that the Lord thy God
is He which goeth over before thee…," Deuteronomy 9:3*

Here is the situation. You are finally headed into the Promised Land. You have caught a glimpse of it. This land is fertile and large. There is plenty of space to settle into. You have seen the fruit of this land. It is rich and abundant. You have also been wandering around in your wilderness for way too long. You might have entered in, let us say…40 years ago, but because of unbelief, you have been led away into the opposite direction. God has definitely been with you, though. You have had a multitude of incidences and reminders that He has never left you. You have had specific signs of His presence, and now you are in sight of the Promised Land. There is a catch, though.

There are Canaanites on your Promised Land! Specifically, they are called Anakims. They are taller than you are. They are stronger than you are. They are financially stable. They have been on this land much longer than you have, so they know the land inside and out. It is now safe to assume that they did not get the divine memo to vacate the premises. They do not know your God, and they do not have the faintest intent on leaving. What happens now?

Do you see yourself in this kind of situation? The name of your land might not actually be called "Canaan," and you may not actually be considered an "Israelite," but you are a child of God, and He has made a promise to you. You are standing painfully close to your promise…close enough to see the enemy fully reclined and at ease on your possession. He is not by any means planning to give up that inheritance that you have been promised. He is bigger, stronger, and he has lived longer than you have. Now, let me repeat my question. What happens now?

Let us go back to the passage because there are a few keys to your victory embedded in the verses of Deuteronomy 9. First, know this: God is fully aware of the enemy and how he has threatened you. He knows that the nations are "greater and mightier" than you are. He knows that the city of promise is presently "fenced up to heaven," (vs. 1). He knows the reputation that precedes the enemy, (vs. 2). God was fully aware of the circumstance when He gave you your promise. As important as these obstacles seem, they have nothing to do with what is about to happen.

There is a reason why God asks us to "walk by faith, and not by sight," (II Corinthians 5:7). By sight, all you see is the threat in front of you. Your senses are inundated with the weight, height, and appearance of the enemy. Your memory is full of vivid accounts of past defeats and apparent failures. According to all the evidences of feeling, the enemy is not about to relinquish your land. But, you walk by faith.

Secondly, know this: "...that the Lord thy God is he which goeth over before thee; as a consuming fire he shall destroy them...," (Deuteronomy 9:3). God goes over before you! By faith, all enemies before you will be subdued. Had the children of Israel actually seen God subdue enemies as large and powerful as the Anakims before? Probably not! But, the secret to victory did not lie in the size, height, or the power of Israel, or the enemy. Such is the danger of making decisions according to what you see instead of Who you know. As the Word says: "Not by might, nor by power, but by my Spirit, saith the Lord," Zechariah 4:6.

God is the One that will subdue the enemy, and you will witness it. Deuteronomy 9:3 says, "He shall bring them down before thy face..." All you will have to do is to "drive them out, and destroy them quickly, as the Lord hath said unto thee." God will do all the tough stuff. You just believe, follow and obey! Nothing is impossible for God. When God took on the responsibility of "bringing the enemy down," He took that burden out of your hands. Now there is no reason why the enemy cannot be driven out of the land. In addition, the phrase "before your face" implies that you will witness the mighty works of God's hands as you carry out His instructions.

Finally, remember this: In Deuteronomy 9: 4-6, God warns us about taking His glory. Do not conclude that the victory was due to some sort of righteousness that you had. "Remember and forget not, how thou provokedst the Lord thy God to wrath in the wilderness..." Do not forget that you are here by grace. You are here and you have overcome because God is good, not you.

God knows your enemies. God made you a promise. God will "bring down the enemy," and when He does, do not steal His glory. "Now, go in to possess nations greater and mightier than thyself, cities great and fenced up to heaven..."

Further Study: *Deuteronomy 8*

Old Man, New Man

"Therefore, if any man be in Christ, he is a new creature; old things are passed away; behold, all things are become new." II Corinthians 5:17

That old man...he's a monster, isn't he? He is who he is. The old man answers to the flesh and does things in the flesh. The old man avoids and evades the things of the Spirit because those things of the Spirit cut the old man to the core. The Spirit will expose the old man for who he is in an effort to show the old man that he needs something much greater than himself. He is destitute.

The old man, in his unhealed state, draws unhealed people around him. I heard it said that you attract what you tolerate. The old man is attracted to what he does not have, so it is true that opposites attract, but it is from an unhealthy perspective. The old man deals in envy, which means that he dwells not in the fact that he can develop in himself what he does not have, but he lives in his emptiness and always envies the person that seems to have what he does not. He is too lazy to develop the necessary skills or qualities that he is attracted to, and, to be honest, it is just easier to hate someone who does have them. So, the old man is surrounded by his own kind, and chained to prisoners of a similar caliber. He hears the "old man" rhetoric from his cellmates every day, so his bondage is often reinforced.

The enemy of souls makes it seem that the life of the old man is the desired life to have, but the old man is miserable, naked, and in need of everything. The old man needs to be transformed. More specifically, the old man needs to die.

The word and life of Christ come into the old man and

begin to cut him to the core. The truths of the Word of God cause the old man to see himself as he is...ugly, wretched, and destitute. The law of God shows the old man that there is no hope for him to become what he desperately needs, except through Christ. The old man must die and every time he hears the Word of God, the old man struggles against it, fights it, and dies a little more.

The Word of God transforms the life. It kills the old man but brings about a new birth in the human being. It brings about a brand-new man — a new man! That new man lives on the merits of what Jesus did and what He is. That new man trusts in what Jesus can do for him. That new man begins to hear the promises in the Word of God and believes them and walks through life in faith in what God can do for him.

The company of the new man is different from that of the old. When that new man surrendered his old life, it immediately put him into conflict with the company that the old man kept. Those old supporters are repulsed by the principles of the new man and they must make a choice. They will yield to the change, or they will be forced to abandon him. The new man, because he is being transformed by the grace of God, begins to call other healed humans to be his company, and attracts others who want healing. He comes to learn the principle of II Timothy 1:7 and comes to understand that he can have all that God meant for him to have. He now dwells in the fullness of God. The good he sees in others is something that will be developed in himself. He does not have to envy other people.

All things become new to the new man. Life is new. Joy is attainable every moment he is alive! The old man fights and longs to come back from the dead, but the old man is DEAD. We do not respond to dead things. The body does not send impulses to dead limbs. It does not wait for a response from them. There is no communication, because it is dead. Therefore, the new man does not consult the old man for advice or outlook on life. The new man does not look for the old man's interpretation of life's experiences...because the old man is dead and will stay dead. The old man has passed away. All things become new!

Gossip

*"The tongue has the power of life and death,
and those who love it will eat its fruit,"* Proverbs 18:21 NIV

God's creatures continue to amaze me. I believe that God has hidden some part of His wisdom in each part of His Creation. Take the honeybee, for instance. This little creature is so interesting, in that once it has found a good source of food, it will fly back to its hive to tell others of the bounty. Upon arrival, the excited little bee will do a dance in the midst of its cohorts, briefing them on the location of the bounty it has found. Those directions are dependent upon the sun's position in the sky, so the dance is in relation to where the sun is above the hive. But, the Earth continues to rotate throughout the day, so that the sun's position is not exactly the same as moments before. Therefore, the little bee's dance actually adjusts and changes as the sun moves forward in its path. The bee is inside the hive doing the dance! Does he know that the sun's position has changed and that he is adjusting his directional dance? Amazing!

There is one other quality about the bees that I want to bring attention to that is intriguing to me. Bees are able to keep the inside of the hive comfortable by maintaining a constant temperature no matter how much the outside temperature changes. They do this to protect the developing larvae, but more so, the queen. If the temperature outside rises and the inside of the hive becomes too hot, the workers use their wings to fan away from the queen to cool her. If it becomes too cool in the winter, the bees pack together and fan toward the queen to keep her warm. Bees' ability to fan with their wings keeps the temperature fairly steady.

In extreme instances, these wings come in handy again. If there is an intruder to the hive such as a larger wasp or another type of bee, stinging them may not be possible. Well, the workers will surround the intruder and do something incredible. They will fan toward the intruder. While that does not seem so deep on the surface, they are actually fanning heat toward the intruder, raising the temperature so much so that they virtually burn the wasp in their midst. The power of their fanning wings is amazing.

I began to realize that we have that same power in our tongues! We have the power to lift people up and cast people down with our mouths. We do not really need to be in their presence to do this either. Have we ever had someone come into our circle of association like our workplace, church, or community group? Something about them does not suit our liking, and we began to talk or speculate. Rumors start and they are passed along from mouth to mouth. Some aspects of our conversation might be true, and some false, but we pass the negative tone along to others until our communication "burns" and disables them, eventually driving them out of our midst. They feel unwanted and despised. They may not be able to put their finger on it, but the atmosphere is against them and they are, in effect, driven out and even emotionally "murdered."

However, the opposite is true, too. I have witnessed communities that have taken in an outsider and utilized the power of the tongue in their favor. They directed their prayers and their love toward the target. When they spoke, they spoke of the target's needs and how they might be met. Perhaps the outsider was unmindful of what was being said, but the atmosphere that was created nurtured the outsider or offender, and provided a setting of healing.

Like the bee, we have the collective power to heal or destroy in the power of our tongue. Psalm 34:13 says, "Keep your tongue from evil and your lips from speaking lies."

Leviticus 19:16 says, "Do not go about spreading slander among your people. Do not do anything that endangers your neighbor's life. I am the Lord." Proverbs 11:13 says, "A gossip betrays a confidence, but a trustworthy man keeps a secret." And James 3:8-10 says, "But no man can tame the tongue. It is a restless evil, full of deadly poison. With the tongue, we praise our Lord and Father, and with it, we curse men, who have been made in God's likeness. Out of the same mouth comes praise and cursing. My brothers, this should not be."

What will you do with the power of your tongue? Will people be healed or destroyed?

Healing

Forgiveness

"And forgive us our debts, as we forgive our debtors."
Matthew 6:12

Hello, mic check. Testing...one...two...three! Is everybody out there still human? Well, if everyone out there is still part of humanity, I have a special message for you. For the rest of your earthly life, you will need two precious keys: Confession and Forgiveness. If you want to live free, you will have to use them on a continual basis from here on out. This passage is about forgiveness.

As long as you are human, you will make mistakes. "There are presently 7.4 billion people (and counting) living in the world. It is a guarantee that at least one of these 7.4 billion people will step on your toes at some point, and you will step on someone else's. Someone will rub you the wrong way and chances are, to some degree, you will resent what happened.

The problem with humans is that we can carry our little garden of resentments throughout life. We do not like being offended or hurt. Resentments can turn to bitterness, and nurtured bitterness can eventually turn to hate. We cannot live this life and avoid being hurt. Some of us were deeply hurt before we were old enough to explain what happened. For others, time does not seem to have healed anything. I have certain memories that I can relive right now and become bitter all over again. Something has to break the cycle; there has to be some way out. Well, here is some great news!

The Greek word for forgiveness is "Aphiemi," apo=from, and hiemi= to send. The denotation of "Aphiemi" becomes "to send away, to dismiss." But, what are we sending away?

When we refuse to forgive someone who has offended us, what are we saying? We are saying that we will not let them off the hook. Why does letting the offender off the hook rankle in our minds so much? The answer is that we do not want them to go free. We want them to suffer for what they have done.

We want them to pay, so we vow not to ever forget what they have done to us. We were wronged, and we will hold them to the guilt of it. We have to, right? How else will they be punished? Here is a suggestion: How about letting God handle it? God says "Vengeance is mine; I will repay...," Romans 12:19. God knows how and when to administer vengeance and punishment; but His approach is always based in love, and ours is based in hurt. Are we sure we can trust God to handle it? He says in Isaiah 55:8, 9 that His ways of doing things are not like our ways. He might not do it the way we want it done. Is that okay, or should we do it ourselves? Let's weigh a couple of options.

We say that we will make the offenders suffer, but who really suffers the most — the offenders or us? Think of what it costs us to hold the offenders to guilt. We always have to remember the offense, so that whenever we see them we can launch the offense at them on demand. That action requires brain space and processing power to be kept in our memory, taking away precious time and energy that can better be devoted to other, more healthy tasks. Some of us have become very good at storing hurtful things, too.

Then there is the "focus" factor. Out of a crowd of people, our offenders need to know that our "good morning" applied to everyone but them. We need to be nice to everyone else except the offender; that requires keen selectivity. We need to be able to turn off our good nature at a moment's notice, just in case they appear somewhere that we did not expect them to, so it virtually requires of us an adaptable split-personality.

Last, but not least, we need to make sure they feel our pain; but honestly, do they ever really feel it? More often it is those we don't mean to target who feel it instead...those who are around us the most. To be successful, our demonstrations of pain need to be more public and the more public, the more risk to innocent bystanders. Yes, it is true. We suffer the most. Look at how much energy it takes to maintain resentment. Soon we become consumed with revenge.

Oh, and let's not forget that God says, "For if ye forgive not men their trespasses, neither will your heavenly Father forgive your trespasses," Matthew 6:15. Now, we really have some dead weight to drag around. Let's total up the tab — we've got daily, guilt-maintenance to do on offenders, and the truckload of our own guilt bearing down on us. No wonder so many of us are knotted up, bent over, and disfigured inside.

When I choose to forgive the person that has wronged me, I let them go free. That's right. I let them off the hook. I am dismissing the guilt and sending it away. I trust God to deal with the offender, and I drop the issue. Drop the issue! Can I really drop the issue? The answer depends on how much I desire to be free. Does forgiveness mean I let myself become a doormat? No. God says in Luke 17:3, "If thy brother trespass against thee, rebuke him." Speak up and let them know that an offense was committed. Does forgiving mean that I will forget what happened to me? Probably not; but, I make it a practice to forgive every time it comes to memory. And, what does God say?

Jeremiah 31:34 says, "...I will forgive their iniquity, and I will remember their sin no more." To "forget" is to be unable to remember. God is able to do all things, right? Does He ever lose the ability to remember something? No. But, He chooses to let the good out-weigh the bad.

I have come to learn that forgiveness is not really for "the other person." It is really for me. I release my own shackles and handcuffs. I undo the knots in my own life. I set myself free to live again. I release the offender to God, and God releases me from guilt. I am twice unburdened. That is also the reason why forgiveness is not based on another's response. Whether they do, do not, or cannot respond positively, that is of no consequence to me. I can still be free.

In light of all this, how often should forgiveness happen? The answer is, it should happen as often as I need to be released. If I am tempted with resentment 50 times in a day, then I need to forgive them in my heart 50 times. Forgiveness is a secret key to personal freedom. How will you use it?

Go Deeper: *Pray this prayer silently with me as often as is necessary. I will lend it to you free of charge!*

"Father, thank You for Your complete and free forgiveness in my life. You have forgiven me of things such as _____. You know that I have held my offender's hostage for reasons such as_____. My list of hostages include _____. Please help me release him/her/them to you now. With Your power, I forgive _____ for what was done to me in advance of my feelings. Please save _____, and please teach me to walk in freedom. Thank You for hearing and answering my prayer, in Jesus' wonderful name! Amen.

Confession

*"Then I confessed my sin and righted what was wrong.
I said, 'I will acknowledge my sins and transgressions
to the Lord and ask Him for forgiveness...'" Psalm 32:5*

We said that there are two keys to freedom that we have been given. Last month we spoke about forgiveness. This month I will speak about confession.

I think back to my childhood, around the third grade. Our little private Adventist school gave us the day off from studying to do what we call "Ingathering," an effort of going into the community to solicit donations for the Church. To make it fun for the kids and to open the hearts of the community, the teachers decided to have the children dress up like Bible characters.

I was staying with my cousins for a few days, whose mother happened to be one of the teachers at the school. I had no access to a Bible costume, so my aunt allowed me to borrow an old towel to wrap around my head. In my mind, I was the spitting image of Moses, and I raced out into the community to gather as much money as people would give me.

On the way back to the school, I realized that in my pursuit of donations I had lost the towel my aunt had entrusted to me. In the time I had left to report back to school, I tried my best to retrace my steps, but it was to no avail. The towel was gone. Overflowing with guilt, I walked through the schoolyard thinking of an excuse for why I had lost the towel. "I was attacked by a dog?" No, that had legal implications! "I was robbed and beaten badly?" No, without a bleeding face, it would be difficult to convince anyone! What would I tell my aunt? I concluded I would avoid the mention of the subject altogether. Maybe my aunt would forget to ask about it! Maybe it would fade into the past as unimportant. Surely, I was not the first to lose a towel. My cousins were always losing things...and punished for it. Oh, no! It was my only hope. I had to avoid the issue.

The ride home from school took about two years...no, really, it did feel like two years. While my cousins chattered excitedly about Ingathering, I hid silently in the corner of the car, because at any moment, I feared my aunt would break through the conversation and interrogate me with questions about the missing towel. That night, I was sure she would give me the third degree for dessert instead of apple pie, or maybe retribution would surprise me in math class the following day. I was a complete wreck waiting for the punishment. I am sure I was more than a little short-tempered and edgy waiting for that fateful moment: like a tree branch waiting to snap from excess weight. The suspense was too much for me...I could not walk another moment on eggshells...I could not sleep another night with one eye open, buried under bed covers. The guilt was eating my insides away, rendering me a hollow shell of a boy.

The next day, I think it was during a rest period at school that I finally snapped. You see, my cousins had a way of peering at me with relentless, inquisitive eyes: something like Chinese water torture. "They are on to me," I thought to myself. In fact, it seemed as though the entire class knew I was hiding a secret. One of my cousins finally broke the silence... "Joey, what's wrong?" In a moment, I burst into tears. Like an inmate at the state penitentiary, I walked the green mile to the front of the room where my aunt's desk was located, escorted by my cousin. With tearful, sobbing words, I finally confessed to my crime. Cowering from the impending judgment, I awaited sentence.

I know my aunt had to have been laughing to herself at some point over my childlike soap opera. I was so intense! After entering my self-induced plea of guilt, she grabbed my shaking hands and described the towel I had lost. It was an old dishtowel that she had stopped using because it was so tattered. She had many more at home. She gave the towel to me because she could afford to let it go in case something like this came up. She expected that I might lose it. I was a child, and children lose things. Forgiveness came swiftly.

With a bit of embarrassment, I got myself together and made my way back to my desk. Like helpless forest creatures mistaken for monsters, my cousins and classmates looked on from their surrounding desks; I felt somewhat silly now.

Had I confessed earlier, I would have avoided the sleepless night and the entire day of guilty preoccupation. I felt as though I had aged about four days with so much worry.

After years of dealing with guilt, I learned that confession is the key that unlocks the handcuffs of guilt and self-condemnation. The power of confession is that (when done honestly) it leads us to the truth. When we submit ourselves to the truth, the truth sets us free. The enemy throws so many faults and mistakes in our faces and vows never to let us forget the wrong we have done. God invites us in I John 1:9 to allow Him to unlock the handcuffs and allow us to run free again. The sad truth is that some of us have become accustomed to carrying guilt around on our shoulders like a dead body, refusing to relieve ourselves of the condemnation. Guilt has become a part of who we are and how we think.

Is confession good for the soul? Absolutely! It is a necessity for the soul to exist in good health. How often must confession happen? It must happen as often as we experience guilt and self-condemnation. I have personally confessed millions of times over the last 20 years. I've confessed to God and to thousands of people that I have wronged.

No matter how long we live, until the Lord comes back, we will always need forgiveness and confession. How can confession set you free?

Go Deeper: Proverbs 28:13; 1 John 1:9, 10

Freedom

> "And the Lord God commanded the man, saying, 'Of every tree of the garden thou mayest freely eat: But of the tree of the knowledge of good and evil, thou shalt not eat of it: for in the day that thou eatest thereof thou shalt surely die.'" Genesis 2:16, 17

In June of 2005, Karly, my daughter was born. Feeling my inadequacy as a parent, I immediately prayed for wisdom on how to raise this bundle of joy. As if it was specifically planned, someone recommended a book called *On Becoming Toddlerwise*. I found this book to be greatly helpful in childrearing, and I quickly began to internalize its principles.

I found one principle particularly interesting to me under the chapter called "Moral Foundations." The principle states, "Your desire for the developmental harmony of your child makes it necessary that you grant freedoms to the child only after he or she attains the age appropriate level of self-control," page 36. Age appropriate self-control is the basis upon which parents should grant freedoms to their children. The authors go on to state this:

> Freedoms greater than self-control = developmental confusion
> Freedoms less than self-control = developmental frustration
> Freedoms equal to self-control = developmental harmony

Let me briefly explain. I create developmental confusion when I let six-month old Karly handle her own "Veggie Tales" DVDs. She yanks them out the casing, drools on them, uses them as a bobsled as she slides across the living room floor, and now they are damaged and unusable. I've given her too much freedom to handle a technology that she has not demonstrated the self-control to properly handle and care for, so I have to forbid her from handling DVDs until she's attained more self-control.

I create developmental frustration when I continue to insist on spoon-feeding my now 19-month old daughter. She has demonstrated that she can handle a children's fork very well, along with other table manners. But, because she's still my little "poopsie-woo" and I just cannot bear to see her grow up so fast, I insist on feeding her. I frustrate her by not allowing her the freedom to feed herself when she has demonstrated self-control to handle her own fork.

Finally, Karly experiences developmental harmony when she exercises self-control necessary to finish all of the vegetables on her plate. I then give her the freedom to enjoy her much-anticipated yellow Popsicle.

Our first parents forfeited the freedom of the Garden of Eden when they relinquished their trust in God concerning that freedom. Without that vital trust, the greater blessings of the Garden would become a curse to them in their selfishness, and so in mercy, the humans were escorted out. Their right to exist in the Garden was revoked; somewhat like my having to take the DVDs from Karly.

I suppose the principle of granted freedoms did not sink into my being until one specific morning when I was talking to God. I had grown increasingly stressed the more I thought about the fact that I had been praying, now, for years that God would deliver me from financial debt. I believed that I was to be the "head and not the tail," Deuteronomy 28:13. And that I was exhorted to "owe no man anything but to love one another," Romans 13:8; but it seemed that financial freedom was not a promise meant for me, and the very thought made me all the more frustrated as I poured out my heart to God.

Quickly and quietly, the response came to me: "Financial freedom is just that...a freedom. It's one that you haven't yet exercised the self-control to handle." Instantly, my spirit was checked. I thought of all the unbalanced checkbooks, the frivolous spending sprees, the many instances of neglected tithes and offerings, and the many small bills left unpaid while I bought gadgetries for myself. I had been an unfaithful steward of God's resources. As a parent of a little child, I finally understood why it would have been silly of God to grant me a freedom that I had not exercised self-control to handle.

It is not that God does not want to give us greater freedoms; He wants us to become faithful stewards of our bodies, our finances, our possessions, our relationships, and the privileges that we already enjoy. Without corresponding self-control, greater blessings become great curses. It only takes a quick glance into society to see freedoms granted to people who do not possess the corresponding self-control to handle them — from the least of us to the greatest. I believe that one day, trusting in the righteousness of Jesus Christ, humans will be granted that freedom to be faithful stewards of the Garden of Eden again.

When we trust in God, He is more than willing to allow us to experience the corresponding freedom.

Go Deeper: Matthew 7:9-11

Ezzo, Gary M.A., & Bucknam, Robert, M.D. *On Becoming Toddlerwise: Parenting the Second Year From First Steps to Potty Training.* Mt. Pleasant, S.C.: Parent-Wise Solutions, Inc., 2003

Turning Up the Heat

"Every man's work shall be made manifest: for the day shall declare it, because it shall be revealed by fire; and the fire shall try every man's work of what sort it is." I Corinthians 3:13

I remember attempting to bake some brownies in the oven one day. I assumed that I had already turned the oven setting to 375 degrees, but I was wrong. After 30 minutes of baking, I returned to the oven to find out that I had left the setting at 200 degrees. I warmed some food in the oven the day before and I had not changed the temperature since then. Needless to say, my brownie masterpiece was partially cooked on the top and completely undone underneath.

I learned that day that when cooking, certain processes are not even activated until the temperature is turned up. Certain combinations of chemical reactions don't occur unless the correct degree of heat is reached. The specified temperatures must be met before the result that I was looking for could be attained. Gold.

In Exodus, Moses had been called and empowered by God to lead His enslaved children out of Egyptian bondage. God gave Moses specific instructions about how to approach Pharaoh and assured him that the first few attempts would not move the hardened heart of the monarch; but first the heat was turned up on the children of Israel.

As Moses and Aaron approached Pharaoh, asking that he let the Israelites go into the wilderness to worship God, Pharaoh flatly refused, just as God said he would. Further attempts were not only met with the same response, but the irritated king went on to conclude that because Moses did not seem to "get his drift," he would turn up the heat in such a way as to subtly heap scathing contempt on Moses and his "God." And turn up the heat he did; for when the Israelites reported to work the next day, they quickly learned about the memo that went out stating that the straw for the bricks to be made would not be provided by Pharaoh any longer. They would be responsible for collecting the raw material and making the brick, and no matter how much more time or energy that task required, they would not be allowed to make one brick less than the normal quota. According to Pharaoh, the extra work should be sufficient to release them from the "evils" of idle thought and daydreaming. For Israel, certain elements of their faith in God could not be activated until the heat of their situation was turned up against them.

So what happens when the heat gets turned up? What happens when the enemy learns of our vows to God and makes the battle official by stirring up the temperature of hell against us? Whenever we are called out of some type of bondage, like the Israelites, or called to leadership, like Moses, there will always be something or someone to contend with the vision. Someone will suggest that we are delusional for leaving the comfort zone...out of touch for hearing the call to something more...foolish for answering the will of God. As long as evil exists, God's wisdom will be foolishness to the world. The enemy would love to have us faint in the ovens of persecution and the heat of the threat. He would love to burn up our dream of freedom and consume our glorious hope. However, when dealing with His children, God views the heat of the trial by fire as a "refining" agent rather than a "consuming" agent (Malachi 3:2, 3). We, then, as children of God, allow the fire to refine us and complete our development of character, as the refiner's fire completes the process of purifying gold and silver.

The accomplished chef is vigilant, but does not worry about whether the heat will do its job on the prized dish because the process of the fire will always work to the will of the chef, preparing the food as no other force can. The accomplished cook ponders only the result that will be brought forth because of the fire...a culinary masterpiece.

Color of Character

"...And His countenance was like the sun shining in its strength." Revelation 1:16

When my daughter Karly was born, she was as pale in complexion as both of her grandmothers, who are very light-skinned. She was an extraordinary work of art that I could not really come to terms with. This was a human being that had been brought into the world! Amazing! But there she was, colorless, except for the red bruise on her forehead where she was lodged on her mother's pelvic bone upon exiting the womb.

When Karly was about 20 minutes old, she experienced her first hair shampoo, which she did not like one bit! Karly cried the most pitiful cry you have heard, and as she cried, the color of her little face turned beet red. Oh, she hollered and wailed, and when she was finally done, her face retained that deeper shade of red. The first diaper change that took place a little while later spawned another outburst of weeping that flushed her skin again. There were many moments of crying that followed in the next few days, weeks, and months coupled with her exposure to the sun that helped Karly's skin tone to settle into a beautiful olive-brown color.

I spent many moments staring at Karly, wondering how her gorgeous skin color could have been divinely predetermined. I had to recall all of the moments of awful crying that seemed to have done nothing more than dispersed blood throughout her body, bringing color with it. I am not sure what she would have looked like had she not cried a tear from birth, but somehow I do not think the pigment would have been activated the way it was had she not been exposed to the stress of weeping.

Can it be possible that exposure to the trials and stresses of life add the most beautiful pigments to our character? Having traveled from city to city with Take 6, I've come back into contact with people I have known in high school and college. I have noticed that there is something different about a person's character or "complexion" when I see them again after years of experience and life. Some have been through the most profound trial and hurt that anyone can experience, and these are the ones that I am most taken by. There is something about the extremes of happiness and sorrow that add "tone" to someone's life. The deeper the sorrow and pain — the more ingrained the application of the lesson learned — the richer the hue of their "spiritual" complexion.

Isaiah 52:14 says that Jesus' life of carrying our pain and sorrow and finally dying on a cross changed His "visage" or appearance so much so that as He hung on the cross He was unrecognizable to men. But the "color" that the suffering and pain added to Jesus' character so much transformed His glorified countenance, that John could only describe it in Revelation 1:16 as shining "like the sun...in its strength."

The key to developing such character is that I determine what attitude I will take toward suffering and pain. Some have allowed trials to destroy their faith in God, as though trials were not supposed to occur. I Peter 4:12, 13 says, "...think it not strange concerning the fiery trial which is to try you, as though some strange thing happened unto you." I decide in my heart that I will learn from the suffering that I experience, and once I take that attitude, every trial then adds some precious aspect to the building of my character and the beautification of my inner "complexion." Today, I continual to marvel at my daughter's beautiful skin color, and I acknowledge the part that the stress of weeping did to add to it.

Take some time today to examine the effect of stress and trial on your life. What has been your response? What changes, if any, do you need to make in your attitude?

Go Deeper: *Isaiah 52:14*

JOEL KIBBLE

Restoration

Death

"Herein is my Father glorified, that ye bear much fruit; so shall ye be my disciples." John 15:8

When I was a little boy, I used to travel with my family to Huntsville, Alabama, to visit my grandmother. Like any other grandmother, she would have many treats that I looked forward to. Specifically, I looked forward to her peach cobblers. Soon after I arrived at her house, I would find myself playing in her backyard around her three peach trees. When those peach trees would yield their increase, she would have peach cobbler, peach preserves, frozen peaches, and peach nectar...all things "peach."

One summer, as we pulled up into the driveway, I noticed that the peach trees were laden with hundreds of peaches. Concluding again, that this was another prosperous "year of the peach." I ran inside and asked my grandmother if we would have all the wonderful peach goodies that we normally have. "No, not this year," was her response. Shocked and amazed, I could not understand why there would not be such a harvest as previous years, especially since there were so many peaches on the trees. My grandmother explained, "I didn't get the opportunity to prune my trees last year, so all the fruit you see is bitter and under developed. Don't be fooled by the multitude of peaches you see!"

I really did not understand the connection between pruning trees and sweet fruit until many years later when my grandmother died. Death seemed to be much more prevalent at this time in my life, as many of my friends and family were being claimed by it. As many humans do, I asked God why He allowed people to die, notwithstanding my prayers to keep them alive. The answer did not become clear to me until moments before I was to sing for my grandmother's memorial service. My thoughts were taken back to the solitude of the peach trees in my grandmother's backyard. Under the shade of those trees, I understood that pruning involves the removal of fruit, excess foliage, and quite often, large limbs. Strangely enough, I did remember coming to my grandmother's house and finding the trees cut back so thoroughly at times, that it seemed they would never grow again; but it was precisely this process that ensured that nourishing sap would be redirected to the limbs that remained.

Sometimes God allows certain "branches" of our family trees to be removed so that those of us who remain may become more fruitful. Many of us are yet bitter and under developed. For some, the fruit of the Spirit is still missing in our lives, and will likely remain this way until certain circumstances or people are gently removed. God has promised that the righteous will be raised incorruptible when Jesus returns, so we will see our loved ones again. Death might mean that we will surely cry sometimes, but it can make us sweeter and further develop our character as surely as pruning a peach tree makes peaches sweet. "Weeping may endure for a night, but joy cometh in the morning," Psalm 30:5.

***Go Deeper:** I Thessalonians 4:13-17; Galatians 5:22, 23*

Self-Worth

"For God so loved the world, that He gave His only begotten Son, that whosoever believeth in him should not perish, but have everlasting life." John 3:16

Having a sense of self-worth is so important. For the lack of self-worth, women and men become prostitutes. For the lack of self-worth, people abandon their families and take the lives of their children. For the lack of self-worth, people will videotape their own suicide to be posted on the Internet. The price of the lack of self-worth can be easily seen in the surrounding tragedies of our society.

All my life, whether I have known it or not, I have searched for self-worth. I was devastated by the rejection of peer groups in elementary and high school — environments where children yearn for acceptance and value. I clung to those who would speak kind words to me. I remained in unhealthy relationships much longer than I should have because I was afraid of being alone.

One of the most exciting and affirming times of my life — joining Take 6 — was followed by a period of six or seven years of bewilderment. Take 6 saw value in me, apparently because they chose me to join the group over so many other more talented singers. I saw my value in their eyes, but I could not see value in myself, for myself. I found myself continually wanting them to tell me what they valued in me.

I chose to become a youth pastor of a church because the senior pastor saw value in what I could bring to his congregation. In fact, I specifically told him that if he could help me decipher the apparent "calling" on my life and help me learn how to pursue it, I would work for him. As it turned out, he simply could not and did not help me learn my value. Again, I looked into his eyes and saw that I brought some type of value to his situation and found myself continually wanting him to tell me what value he saw in me, but I didn't know it for myself.

The intrinsic defect in looking to others to give me my value is that the success of my search is subject to humans, who are searching for value themselves. They see value according to how they are benefited. So if they happen to be having a bad day, identifying your value will be suspended until further notice.

In vain, we search and pursue self-worth, and overlook the only One who really knows what our value is, and Who can really speak to us about it. Apparently, He values us so much that it was worth Him suffering the worst punishment at the hands of men that anyone has suffered, and dying so that we could begin to understand that infinite value! Would not the Creator know the value of His creation? More than that, would not the Redeemer know the value of the objects that He gave so much to redeem?

I was blessed to see my daughter brought into this world. She was born with a heart condition that I could not do anything about. I would have gladly given my heart for hers because her value to me is so immeasurable. It would hurt me if my daughter were to subject herself to some other unsatisfied human being, basing her entire value system upon their fleeting opinion of how she could benefit them. I am just a human, earthly father. How much more does God infinitely love and value my daughter? Or the rest of His children?

Purpose

"But the very hairs of your head are all numbered."
Matthew 10:30

Anyone who has been to my house has met one of my two dogs, the silver female Miniature Schnauzer named Penelope. She is my personal, high-spirited little guardian that follows me all over the house. Penelope has a distinctive look when groomed properly. Her traditional features and her majestic stance make me wonder whether I should have raised her as a show dog. Lately, though, the local groomers in my vicinity have butchered her haircuts causing me to be less than impressed with her looks, to say the least, so I decided to move in a more positive direction.

I decided to call the American Miniature Schnauzer club to find a local chapter. Nashville, Tennessee didn't have one, but I was directed to some local breeders. I called one of them to ask whom they might see for grooming, since I knew that they might take their dogs' appearance seriously. The breeder I spoke to was a kind gentleman who lived in Nashville. After relating my frustration to him, he laughed and informed me that he also takes the grooming of his dogs seriously. "A great sign!" I thought. He then informed me that he has his dogs shown in competitions quite frequently. "Another great sign!" I exclaimed. He then asked me an interesting question, "What type of cut are you interested in? A normal one or a show cut?" Not really knowing the difference, but always being one to choose the "deluxe" option, I answered, "The show cut, of course!" The gentleman paused, and then responded, "You know that the two cuts are very different, don't you? I decided to be honest and admit that I did not really know the difference.

The breeder shared with me that a show cut involves quite a process. But, before explaining, he gave me a little history on the origin of the Miniature Schnauzer. German farmers, for the purpose of catching vermin such as mice, rats, and rodents, bred the Schnauzer many years ago. The breed originally possessed not one, but two coats: the inner coat, a soft downy layer, and the outer coat, a coarse exterior. My Penelope only had a soft downy silver coat, with sparse, random strands of coarse dark gray hair positioned here and there. The breeder informed me that without this second outer coat, a Miniature Schnauzer could never be admitted into a competition. Well, there go my chances for my little secret champion! The breeder continued by saying that to show this breed of dog requires that they must go through a process of being "stripped" for a competition. Stripping involves the literal pulling out of all the hair around the entire body excluding the legs. "All the hair?" "Actually pulling it out?" I asked in disbelief. "The whole body, except for the legs," the breeder assured me. "And it requires a few weeks' time to accomplish, as the hair must be pulled out in sections. It takes about 8 to 12 weeks to grow back completely before it is then cut into shape," the gentleman continued. "I know it seems harsh, but if the dog was serving its original purpose in its historic environment around a farm, the weeds and briars would naturally pull out the hair as the dog runs through them. Because the dog does not presently operate in its original purpose, the hair must be physically pulled out to achieve the second coat. You cannot get past that first coat by simply shaving it off with clippers."

Suddenly, I was glad I did not let my ignorant pride allow my dog to be plucked like a chicken. After I opted for the "normal" cut, the breeder gave me information for a groomer located about an hour from me who prepares many of the dogs that are shown in Tennessee. That afternoon, I asked myself a couple of questions:

Am I operating according to my original purpose? What was I created to do for God? I wonder if there are hints of more profound characteristics about me that cannot be developed and perfected without stress and trial. What about those objectionable traits of character that keep my spiritual growth stunted?

Have I gone past my first coat? What will it take to strip away that externalism that I use to impress people? If I were walking within my godly purpose, would the process itself serve to strip away the externalism? Is there an easier way to strip away the superficial without pain and stress?

Do I appreciate the process of time? Processes involve time and steps toward the result. Am I trying to rush the process? If so, would I be satisfied with the results?

Finally, (and I have to laugh at this one) have I ever seen any bald Schnauzer show dogs?

Let me explain. We fear the pain and humiliation of being stripped by God, but He has never failed to uproot any evil trait in our lives that needed to go, and He has never pulled out any godly trait that was not meant to grow back more abundantly. I have never seen a bald Schnauzer whose hair never grew back from enduring the stripping process. Moreover, if God "numbers the very hairs on my head," Matthew 10:30, I am sure He is careful enough not to pull more than I can bear at one time (I Corinthians 10:13).

I have to trust whatever means God uses to bring out my "second coat." Whatever needs to happen so that He can "show" me to the world, I will endure and accept. I choose to walk in my God-ordained purpose.

Pull Harder: Hebrews 12:6, 11

The Blessing of Job

"Then Job arose, and rent his mantle, and shaved his head, and fell down upon the ground, and worshipped..." Job 1:20

During my life on this Earth, I have experienced two stock market crashes where people have lost all their wealth overnight. I have heard stories a few times about investors who had lost all and jumped out of windows, committing suicide. They apparently had nothing more to live for than wealth, and when that was taken away, they ended it all. I have heard stories about the aftermath of the 9/11 disaster on the United States and its effect on the U.S. economy. I have heard stories about people who, after years of saving and investing money in their 401Ks, lost all of its worth in a matter of months. A lifetime of saving in this turbulent day and age was devalued in such a short period of time.

But, few have had to experience the one-two "punch" that Job had to experience. The devil challenged God by suggesting that Job's fidelity was only founded upon the fact that he had always had God's "hedge" of protection around him. "Thou hast blessed the work of his hands, and his substance is increased in the land. But put forth thine hand now, and touch all that he hath, and he will curse thee to thy face," Job 1:10, 11. Suddenly all of Job's material goods were fair game. In a matter of moments, it was all taken away. Job received the awful news that Sabeans had stolen all his cattle and asses, and then killed all the keepers except the one who got away to tell Job of his loss. "While he was yet speaking," another lone servant escaped the unnatural storm of lightning that burned up all of Job's sheep and killed all the servants. Before he had a chance to finish talking and while the second servant stood in amazement, a third lone survivor burst into the room, bloodied and bruised explaining that three bands of Chaldeans stole all the camels and killed all the servants keeping them. To put the dreadful icing on the cake, the third servant was interrupted by a fourth servant that burst into the room to tell a pale-faced Job the unbelievable news that while all his beloved children were eating and drinking, a violent storm exploded upon their house, causing it to fall on all his children, killing them instantly. Of course, he was the only one that escaped to tell the story.

A matter of moments for Job wiped out all his wealth and posterity — within moments of one day. Many would expect Job to do just what the unfortunate investors had done after the market crashes. But, God knew something they did not. Job's self-identity and worth was not wrapped up in what he had. These few purging moments proved it. We identify who we are these days by what we have — a large house, a car of status, a prestigious job with benefits, our marriages, and kids — who are lawyers, doctors, politicians. Somewhere along the way, all these things become who we are. Our worth is wrapped up in what we have instead of Whose we are. If these are taken away, we have nothing more to live for and we blame the world and God for what happened to us. The Word says Job did something unbelievable to our day: He "rent his mantle," "shaved his head," dropped down to his knees and worshipped God. Worshipped God? Where did that come from? Had not God allowed all this to happen? Did not God have ultimate control over all this? Was not Job faithful by offering sacrifices for his children just in case they may have "cursed God in their hearts?" (Job 1:5). This is the way God repays him?

Job dropped down to his knees and worshipped God because his identity was wrapped up in God. His faith was so strong and steadfast because He knew God was God in prosperity and in adversity. God deserved no less praise in adversity than He did in prosperity. Job lost sight of self and did not waste a moment in self-pity. He worshipped God after the worst day of his life. That came from an inner reality that God wishes all His children to have. God was Job's everything. God knew He could take the material possessions that Job had because the relationship was stronger than the blessings. Satan was shown to be the liar that he is.

Is your relationship stronger that your blessings? Where would you stand if everything was taken away? Could you say, "The Lord gave, and the Lord hath taken away; blessed be the name of the Lord?" (Job 1:21).

Little Lad's Lunch

"There is a lad here, which hath five barley loaves, and two small fishes: but what are they among so many?" John 6:9

A young boy wakes up early in the morning. He prepares himself for the day, but he is not going to play with his friends as on other days. On this day, he wants to do something different. An amazing teacher has been speaking near the region of the boy's village, and he wants to hear Him. When considering all the trouble that kids are known to get into over the ages, I imagine that the boy's mother definitely did not mind him going to hear a lecture or two, so she did what any mother would do. She examined to see if his face was clean, and she packed him a small lunch of five loaves of bread and a couple of sardine-sized fish — just in case he got hungry. Wrapping these and placing them in a basket, mother kissed her little boy goodbye, and saw him off down the road as she began another day of toil.

The lad had to move quickly as he saw the swelling crowds headed for the mountain where the Great Teacher was rumored to be. He had to have the best "seat in the house," so he daringly pushed all the way through the crowd until one of the Teacher's guards beckoned him to go no further. "Give the Teacher room, son," the disciple commanded. This was far enough for him, for he now could hear every word that came from the Teacher; and hear every word, he did. So engrossed was the little boy, so engaging were the words of the Great Teacher, that when he finally stood up to stretch, he found the sun setting over the distant hills! Never had he been so enraptured with the teachings of another human!

He wanted to hear even more...any other words that the Teacher could be speaking. He noted the look of perplexity on the face of the disciples, as they seemed to be scanning the crowd of people behind him. He strained to hear their conversation: "...must be hungry...not enough food...over five thousand people..." For the first time that day, the boy looked behind him and eyed a tightly packed sea of people descending the side of the mountain. Maybe the Teacher was hungry and could not get to any food. The boy had all but forgotten his little lunch that had been left unattended all day. It was small, but was it enough to give the Great Teacher something to snack on? It was! Quickly, the boy moved up to the distressed disciple the others called "Andrew." Often ignored, as little boys are, he found that he had to bombard Mr. Andrew, as little boys do, just to present his little lunch to the Teacher. With a quick reply, "That's nice of you...thanks, kid!" Andrew handed the lunch to the Master, and then he eyed the sea of people and sighed, "But what is this among so many?"

The next events followed quickly. The announcement spread through the crowd. "Please be seated, everyone...please!" There was a blessing, then a shuffling, but the boy could not get a good view of what was happening amidst the movements of the men surrounding the Teacher. Was he eating the lunch? Did he like it? Back and forth the men moved. Food was being passed to the little boy to be passed to those behind him. "They must have found someone with a bigger basket," the boy thought. He kept passing food, though. After about half an hour, he saw others around him eating, so he began to eat. The food kept passing by, and then after a while, it began coming back. "Gather up the fragments!" the boy heard. Baskets were passed forward and pieces of fish and bread were deposited. Seeing that the crowd began to be dispersed, the boy got up and prepared to return home, when he felt a hand on his shoulder. It was Mr.

Andrew. "Son, we appreciate your lunch. That was very generous of you. You're going to need some help though, because I am not sure that you are able to carry 12 baskets by yourself, are you?" The boy blushed. Andrew continued, "Where do you live?" "Oh, and the Master said to tell you, 'Thank you.'" "He won't forget your kindness."

Understandably, when mother saw the group of men standing in the front door with her son late in the evening, she had some reason for concern. Even more appalling, though, were the 12 large baskets of food they brought in. "Sit down, Mom," the little boy exclaims, "You're not going to believe this!"

Go Deeper: John 6:1-15

What Doest Thou Here?

"...What doest thou here...?" I Kings 19:9

Have you ever found yourself in a place in life where you knew you were not supposed to be? Have you ever purposely detoured from a path you knew you were supposed to take? This was the very situation that Elijah created for himself when he chose to run from Jezebel.

Elijah's life was most powerful and full of purpose. He was called of God to warn his people that judgment was to fall in the form of famine if they continued in idolatry (I Kings 17:1). He was covered with divine protection while he delivered that scathing message to the wicked king Ahab. He was miraculously hidden from the king's wrath and provided for (v. 3, 4). When the famine had done its three-and-a-half years of work to get Israel's attention, he was sent back to Israel and Ahab to initiate a showdown between the wicked priest of Baal and the Almighty God (I Kings 18:19). He stood alone as the spokesman for Jehovah as God answered his sacrifice by fire, condemning the wicked priests of Baal to death (I Kings 18:20-40). He was the minister of mercy to Israel as God unlocked the barren heavens in a heavy downpour of rain (I Kings 18:41-45). He was even given inhuman strength to run before the king's royal chariot through the rain, down Mount Carmel to the city (v. 46).

Falling asleep from exhaustion after a full day of victory, Elijah was abruptly awakened outside the city gates to the threat of Jezebel's wrath over her slain priests. Not only was she not moved by the identification of the only true God, much less changed in heart by that knowledge, but also, she put her own life on the line to make sure Elijah would not live to see another day. With disap-pointed hopes, Elijah dropped his servant off at a nearby town and ran as fast and as far as he could from the wrath of the evil queen.

Ultimately, Elijah ended up at Horeb, the "mount of God." (I Kings 19:8) As Elijah settled himself into the cave, the word of the Lord came to him and inquired, "What doest thou here, Elijah?" (v. 9) God has a knack for posing questions that He already knows the answers to. God called Elijah to warn Ahab as well as to hide himself at the brook Cherith afterward. God directed him to stay with the widow of Zarephath to be a blessing to her and her son during the awful famine. God redirected him after three-and-a-half years to return to Ahab for the showdown on Mount Carmel, but by whose orders was Elijah to flee from Jezebel into the wilderness?

Has the question ever been posed to you, "What are you doing here?" If so, how do you answer that question? First, be honest. After a steady downturn of income with Take 6 over a period of a couple of years, I found myself applying for a job at a local hardware store. I knew I could not maintain the job and be available to sing with the group, but I needed money badly, and I felt that I had to do something. My bills were a couple of months behind and all my bank accounts were overdrawn. I felt like God was failing me. After driving to a vacant parking lot, I literally "cried" unto God. Moments before I was about to charge Him with "failure to provide," the thought came to me that I had been an awful manager of my finances. I had not so much as balanced my checkbook in years. Each episode presented to me proved God correct, and in desperation, I pleaded for His mercy. God was right, and I had to be honest with myself. I was the one in default.

Second, be willing. I did take a two-week job working construction with my uncle in Huntsville, Alabama, in the interim. During that time, I worked my fingers to the bone (which I did not mind), but I had quite a bit of time for reflection in the hot Alabama sun to contemplate my position in life. Suddenly the question, "What doest thou here?" I realized that though the work was graciously offered to me, this was not what I was called to do. I was reminded of what I was called to do. It was to encourage people through devotions, music, and speaking...something I was commissioned to do a few years ago, but that I had failed to finish. I had to be willing to go back to where I was originally called to labor. Needless to say, after stepping on rusty nails, tetnus shots, bee stings, skin and heat rashes, near misses with poisonous snakes, and dust so far up my nose that my very thoughts seemed soiled, I was ready to return to God's will for me.

When God asks you "What doest thou here," be honest with Him and yourself, and be willing to obey the instructions that follow. God will give you the right perspective, and set you on the right course, as He did Elijah. "Go, return...," I Kings 19:15.

Let Me Fix It

"If you then, who are evil, know how to give good gifts to your children, how much more will your Father in heaven give good things to those who ask Him!" Matt. 7:11

My daughter loves to do crafts. There seem to be few joys that are more inviting than grabbing some craft paper, glue, tape and sparkles and going to town on a new creation. I will often find projects that she's been working on and I'm amazed that she could come up with such ideas. Well, the other day I found something that my daughter had left in the study that made me think. While she was at her mother's house, I came into my study and found the turquoise blue toothbrush holder, that should have been in the bathroom, sitting on her worktable. She apparently had dropped and broken the top that holds the toothbrushes, as it was separated from the shaft that held it. She had applied scotch tape to reconnect the top to the shaft, but the tape had failed to hold the large piece in place and there it was, partially hanging to the side in an awkward fashion.

At first, I thought to reprimand her for not telling me about the broken toothbrush holder, concluding that she had attempted to keep this a secret from me. We've had a few conversations in the past about keeping secrets to hide mistakes. In fact, I did recall hearing an object strike the floor the day before, but I was preoccupied with something else and didn't follow up on the noise. Her ensuing silence should have been an indicator that something was up, and this was it! But then I thought about what she might have been feeling that caused her to decide to try to fix it herself.

I reflected on my childhood. How many times had I broken

my father's objects and tried to hide them, only to be found out and reprimanded hours, or even days later? How many times had I been suddenly called in from playing with my friends to answer for some mistake I had hoped would never resurface again? A broken trophy? A scratched record? A chewed-up cassette still tangled in the tape recorder? (Um, Am I dating myself?) The lumpy throw rug in the living room of my father's house would betray the many lists of items I've broken and brushed up under that rug, hoping they'd never be found. So, I could easily imagine what she might have been feeling in her effort to conceal her mistakes.

As I stood in the door contemplating, I also thought that this might have been the reason why I've had such low tolerance for her decision to hide things from me. I see it in her because I see it in myself. My desire to hide my brokenness causes me to learn to lie and to place the blame on other people. It's all too familiar to me and it comes from my desire to hide what's broken in my life.

My heart went out to my daughter when I thought about the little bit of stress she might have been going through that caused her to try to fix the toothbrush holder all by herself. But I didn't need her to fix it. I would happily have done it for her. As I bonded the two broken pieces together with superglue, I longed to tell Karly that I found her mistake and that she didn't need to hide it from me. Things break. We all make mistakes, but I wanted her to come to me about it instead of trying to conceal it and fix it herself. Her desire to repair it herself came from an honest place, but I longed to give her the peace of mind that I didn't hold her foible against her.

So, maybe this is how God thinks about us. He knows we make mistakes and He sees that we screwed up. He knows we can't fix what's really wrong in our lives, and never expected us to do so all by ourselves. So maybe He looks at our pitifully patched lifework and has the same tender regard for us. He longs to relieve our stress and release us from the guilt we've been carrying. What do you think? Maybe we should let Him have it. Maybe we should let Him fix it.

Fire!

"How happy is the one whose transgression is forgiven, whose sin is covered!" Ps.32:1

I have a close friend who shared a story with me about a catastrophe that he'd experienced recently. He had a mechanic come over to his house to change a fuel pump in his truck. In order to accomplish this, the mechanic needed to remove the fuel tank to get to the pump and replace it, then replace the fuel tank. My friend asked the mechanic if he needed to pull the truck out of his garage to do this, and the mechanic replied that it wasn't necessary. He would be able to do all that he needed to do from inside my friend's garage.

The mechanic had removed the tank, replaced the pump and was reinstalling the fuel tank when suddenly everything caught fire. In seconds, the garage was engulfed in flames as the calamity rapidly descended into chaos. The mechanic and his assistant whose clothes also caught fire escaped with their lives and miraculously weren't burned. The truck was totally destroyed, though, as was the garage. The fire hadn't reached the rest of the house, but the house was lost to smoke damage, and when the fire department arrived, by protocol, all the windows in the house needed to be smashed out to keep the fire from consuming the structure of the house. The remainder of the house also sustained water damage, which rendered it completely unlivable. In a matter of seconds, everything my friend owned was damaged.

Blessings? Absolutely. I won't go into the fact that he, his wife, his mother-in-law, and his children were all away from home on this particular day, and that most of the rooms they usually occupied were closest to the garage. That's another testimony. What intrigued me was what the fire marshal stated as the most probable cause for the start of the fire. While the mechanic appeared to have known what he was doing, it was determined that the garage wasn't a sufficiently ventilated area, even with the doors wide open. The mechanic and his assistant had been working and had become familiar and unmindful of the trapped gasoline fumes that surrounded them. From a most unlikely source, a spark had ignited the trapped fumes. Positioned in the garage was a refrigerator and its motor had automatically turned on, producing a spark sufficient to ignite the trapped fumes, setting the truck and the garage on fire.

For some reason, I couldn't stop thinking of this fact, even though my friend went on to testify to the goodness of God in restoring what the fire had taken. The unfortunate events ironically strengthened his relationship to his wife and gave him a greater sense of the blessedness of life and its value.

Meditating over this event during the next couple of days, it became clear to me. "Joey, you have been praying for more and more of the Holy Ghost's fire and Its presence in your life, but like the mechanic, there have been some potentially dangerous, surrounding conditions that you haven't been mindful of or seriously considered."

Though he was able to do the job and had undoubtedly done it many times before, the mechanic had become familiar in his skills and had neglected basic fundamental rules. He shouldn't have been working in an unfamiliar environment with potentially hazardous appliances. He should have chosen a well-ventilated environment, such as a properly equipped, professional auto-mechanic garage. He had great intentions, but intentions alone were not sufficient to substitute for obedience to general rules of safety.

In the book of 2 Samuel 6, there was a story in the Bible about God's people becoming equally careless of their environment. David wanted to bring the ark of God back into the camp of Israel after they had become lackadaisical with the symbol of God's abiding presence. Their enemies, the Philistines, had snatched the ark from the Israelites, which had become nothing more than a glorified charm to them. While the ark, of itself, did nothing to win the victory for the Israelites, it desecrated the Philistine's land and became a catastrophe wherever it was placed while in their possession. In desperation, the Philistines put the symbol of God's presence on a cart led by cattle and turned it loose, figuring that if the cattle miraculously pulled it out of their land and took it, unguided, back to the land of Israel, it must be the result of divine providence.

King David had good intentions of putting the ark back where it belonged, but He and his priestly leaders had become familiar with disregarding what God had asked. According to the book, Patriarchs and Prophets, Uzzah the priest stretched out his hand to steady the ark that was being carried on a cart back to Israel and was killed for touching it. There were three reasons given. One, Israel had become used to sin and disregarded God in a number of areas, which was how the ark got stolen in the first place. Israel didn't follow His express commands and had fallen out of vital communion with Him yet decided to bring the symbol of His presence out to wave it around in front of their enemies as though it had intrinsic power apart from God Himself.

Two, God wanted it transported in a particular manner that He spelled out to the priests. The ark was constructed with rings attached to its sides, in which staves were inserted and it was to be "borne," or carried on the priest's shoulders; not pulled by a cart. (Ex. 25:14) Uzzah, as a priest of the Lord, should have remembered this fact, but he didn't think it important what God had said about how it should be carried.

"God should be happy enough that we're simply bringing it back," he might have thought.

Three, Uzzah was saturated with sin in his life and presumed to approach the symbol of the Almighty to touch that which is holy to God. The only time a priest even entered into the immediate presence of God was when the high priest entered the most holy place, once a year, to atone for the sins of the Israelites. But priest and people had become familiar with unbelief, disregarding God's specific instruction on the transportation of the ark. Israel and Uzzah felt comfortable in doing what seemed a well-intended task and doing it their way. So, God dealt with him, and spared all of Israel in mercy to show them He meant business.

As I listened to the details about how the fire started, the Lord made it clear to me that lately, I've been praying for more and more of the fire of the Holy Ghost. That prayer has become routine, really, but I've grown immune to the sense of what it means to be fully inhabited by the Holy Spirit. Ps. 32:1 says, "Blessed is the man...whose sin is covered." I've become comfortable moving about before the presence of God with open sin in my life, not considering how much He abhors sin or how He goes to great lengths to separate me from it by having His own innocent Son die for "my" disobedience, and not realizing that to sin, His very presence is a "consuming fire." (Heb. 12:29) Yes, He wants to inhabit me and fill me with more of His abiding presence. Jesus has embodied my sin and has suffered my penalty, so that I can live my life through Him. Not believing this truth causes me to "put forth my hand" like Uzzah, in an attempt to right what is wrong in my life. That sin of unbelief is as flammable as gasoline fumes, and God's mercy is the reason I'm not consumed. Good intentions are not a substitute for obedience.

David and the rest of Israel were spared despite the damages; the mechanic and his assistant were spared despite the damages; I have been spared despite the damages, and all because God wants me to believe. "...For this is good and acceptable in the sight of God our Saviour; Who will have all men to be saved, and to come unto the knowledge of the truth." (1 Tim. 2:3,4)

JOEL KIBBLE

Empowerment

David

"Now Eliab his oldest brother heard when he spoke to the men; and Eliab's anger was aroused against David, and he said, 'Why did you come down here? And with whom have you left those few sheep in the wilderness? I know your pride and the insolence of your heart, for you have come down to see the battle.' And David said, 'What have I done now? Is there not a cause?'" I Samuel 17:28, 29 NKJV

In every area of life, there is a cause. For every cause, there is a David. For every David, there is a Goliath. For every Goliath, there is a stone.

In every area of life, there is a cause.

Whatever the area of life you represent, there will always be a need and an opportunity for integrity and courage to be walked out. The business sector needs men and women of strong values to conduct honest business. The music industry needs committed artists who live what they sing about. Families today need parents who are dedicated to raising godly seed. Society needs single men and women, boys and girls, who are not afraid to stand up for what they believe. It does not matter what part of society you characterize — a need will make itself known within your sphere of influence.

For every cause, there is a David.

For every need, God has prepared a David with the training, the tools and the character necessary to meet that need. God may have raised you in the most uninhabited of circumstances, completely outside the scope of the masses, tending the most humble of responsibilities, but as surely as He is God, you are definitely equipped for the job. You must understand that the masses are trained to look for the "Saul" type of leaders. These leaders are the ones who look and talk like a leader should, speak the kind of words that you would expect a leader to say, and appear to have the material possessions that you would expect a leader to have. The masses look for external qualifications.

"... For the Lord does not see as man sees; for man looks at the outward appearance, but the Lord looks at the heart," I Samuel 16:7. One of the experiences of "David" is that you have probably been overlooked many times. David did not get the memo from his own father that a prophet of God wanted to meet with all the brothers (I Samuel 16:11). While all the "potentials" were lined up before the prophet, the "nonessentials" were tending sheep way out in the fields. David was overlooked by his own family!

God knows who you are when no one else does because He reads character. Character is who you are behind closed doors. God knows that the qualities of a leader are grown internally and demonstrated externally. God was looking for this kind of character. He found David.

For every David, there is a Goliath.

There will always be someone, somewhere, who stands ready to challenge and defy the call that God has placed on your life. Someone will always be prepared to cast doubt on the vision that you have been given. There will always be some towering circumstance that rises at the beginning of the day, positions itself within earshot of you and those around you, with the sole purpose of thundering its insults at you and your God. As long as there is an adversary who "walks about like a roaring lion, seeking whom he may devour," I Peter 5:8, there will be giants to deal with. And, as long as you are ready to make a difference or address a need, the giants will be headed your way. Expect them, but know this..."Greater is He that is in you, than he that is in the world," I John 4:4. David knew this. It did not really matter how much larger Goliath was, how heavy his armor was, or how many MORE fingers and toes he had than David. David had on the whole armor of God (Ephesians 6:10-18). The fact was that God was with David; against the God of the universe, everything and everybody was terribly outmatched. When David was questioned about his ability to meet the challenger, his response was this: Size does not matter. Be it a lion, a bear, or an overgrown human, God is God. (I Samuel 17:34-36) The same Power that caused David to defeat these ravenous animals is the same that would defeat the giant...hands down. Because...

For every Goliath, there is a stone.

The Bible says that David and the Israelites stood on one mountain, while the Philistines and Goliath stood on the opposite mountain with a valley in between (I Samuel 17: 3). To get to Goliath, David had to pass through the valley. We will all have to pass through our valley experiences. We would love to stay on the mountaintop, but the light you receive from your mountain top experiences must be walked out in the valleys of life. God promises that even if the valley is overshadowed with death, He is with us (Psalm 23:4). What we sometimes miss, though, is that we find our stones in the valley. Every time we pass through a valley experience, God gives us some principle, some truth, and some revelation about Him that serves as another weapon to kill the giant that will follow. We then do what God has already trained us to do. While David obeyed God — humbly tending the sheep — God was giving him the skills necessary to slay giants. David simply did what he was trained to do for all of his young years, and God put the muscle behind the rock. At what point the rock picked up speed and velocity while sailing through the air, I am not sure, but by the time it connected with Goliath, the force of the rock's momentum caused it to hit and sink into the head of the giant...a sudden, massive concussion; then, for Goliath, lights out!

Remember, in every area of life, there is a cause. For every cause, there is a David. For every David, there is a Goliath. And for every Goliath, there is a stone.

"Yea, though I walk through the valley of the shadow of death, I will fear no evil, for You are with me; Your rod and Your staff, they comfort me," Psalm 23:4.

Go Deeper: *I Samuel 17*

Courage

"Have I not commanded you? Be strong and courageous. Do not be terrified; do not be discouraged, for the Lord your God will be with you wherever you go." Joshua 1:9

According to *Merriam-Webster's Dictionary*, fear is described as "an unpleasant often strong emotion caused by anticipation or awareness of danger." Fear takes on many different faces. There is fear of financial ruin, fear of being alone, fear of loss, fear of death, fear of being exposed, fear of being hurt, fear of rejection, and fear of being uncomfortable, just to name a few. Fear has no respect of age, gender, religion, or nationality. Fear can and will effect anyone. Some may be able to verbalize their fears and some may not. Whether we can or cannot verbalize it, everyone is exposed to some form of fear in this lifetime.

Many of the decisions we make in this life can be based upon avoiding some fear that threatens us. We may marry for fear of being alone; we may choose a particular line of work as a career for fear of being financially destitute and not necessarily because we enjoy that field of study; we put locks on our doors and alarms in our cars for fear of being robbed. Some of us even choose Heaven for fear of hell. Whoever you are, the threat of fear is real.

According to *Merriam-Webster's Dictionary*, courage is described as "mental or moral strength to venture, persevere, and withstand danger, fear, or difficulty." Someone who is defined as "courageous" is often thought of as one "who has no fear." We consider courageous soldiers who march head-on into battle to be — "fearless." We call our generals and heroes "fearless leaders." These brave souls are many times described as those who "lack fear," and we have come to believe that to have courage, all fear must be removed.

    I have often prayed that God would remove all fear so that I could finally have the courage He asks of me. Many more times than not, I have felt those prayers to have gone unanswered. Then one day late last year it began to dawn on me that courage is what you exercise in the face of fear, not in the absence of fear. I have known for a while that I needed to release a devotional corner for Take 6. About this time last year, I began writing devotions in anticipation of releasing them on Take 6's website. As the vision opened up, I began thinking about writing a devotional book, so I looked for an editor. I engaged in the process of writing, editing, correcting and rewriting, knowing that one day I would release my first devotional. I decided to save up at least 50 devotional passages before releasing the first one on the website. All the while, time was passing by and not one had been posted. Alvin Chea kept coming to me and asking me when I would be ready to release a devotional thought, and I kept telling him that I was "in the process." After a year of supposedly writing, preparing, editing, and putting away, I noticed that my creativity was drying up. I soon had nothing to write about as I stared at the computer. After months of praying for answers and getting none, the Lord began to show me that all my preparation, though good in itself, was actually serving to cover for my root issue; I was afraid. What if people didn't feel me? What if readers compared my devotional corner to Alvin's already successful Bass Lines? What if I committed to doing a devotional every month only to come up blank on the deadline? If that happened, how many people would I disappoint? Was I really ready to take on that commitment?

    Around January 13, 2004, I was finally impressed to simply write what was on my heart and post it on the website. What about my fears? No threats had been removed. I could still be very much rejected. One thing was certain, though. If I waited any longer for my fears to dissipate, I would lose the vision. This was my second chance, and I was not going to blow this one. As I began to write, thoughts began to flow again and before I knew it, the devotional was ready.

That night, I began to meditate on the whole experience. God had not removed the element of fear because it was the presence of fear that made courage what it needed to be. Courage is at its best in the very face of fear. If there is no threat and no risk, what need is there for courage? In fact, the greater the threat of fear, the greater the exercise of courage required to move forward. As I prayed for courage, God permitted me to feel enough fear to produce the amount of courage I desired. God had, indeed, answered my prayers after all!

In what parts of your life does courage need to be walked out? In the coming days, meditate on courage and then ask the Lord to help you readdress your fears. Remember, the deeper your fears, the greater the courage God desires for you to exercise. God has made all His promises and resources available to you to back you on your decision, but you must make the first move. The victory is already yours.

Go Deeper: II Timothy 1:7, Psalm 31:24, Deuteronomy 31:6

Focus

"For as he thinketh in his heart, so is he." Proverbs 23:7

I was going through a rough time in my life when a close friend called and shared an experience with me. He told me that in Florida, near one of the theme parks, there is a NASCAR racing facility. This track is special because, if you pay the fee, you will be assigned an instructor that will actually teach you how to drive a stock car like the professionals.

According to my friend, you gear up and you are placed in the driver's seat. Your instructor sits beside you in what would be a passenger's seat holding nothing but a little control box with four buttons. You get strapped in with a helmet and protective gear, and after a thorough orientation you drive out to the track. The first objective is to get you acclimated to high speeds, so after a few laps around, you are instructed to step on the gas. The thrill is indescribable as you find yourself roaring around the oblong track at 90, 100, 110, and 120+ mph! You begin to understand as never before what type of focus champions must have as they weave in and out of the competition that you do not have on your solitary run.

The passing sights become an interwoven blur when, without warning, the instructor hits one of the buttons on that little insignificant box in his lap. Each button corresponds to the hydraulics on each of the four wheels and as a button is pressed, the hydraulics raise a particular wheel, making it slightly higher than the other three. Ultimately, you lose control of the vehicle as this action consequently sends you into a wild, dizzying spinout toward the wall at

120+ mph. You freak out completely as the world whirls around you and life flashes before your eyes, knowing that at any moment you will smash violently into the wall, certainly killing both you and your instructor. Suddenly, the instructor reaches over and grabs your helmet. As if the death spin is not enough, you now wonder whether you have been assigned a lunatic as an instructor, but with both hands, he forces your head in the direction that the car is supposed to go, not where the car is taking you. It takes a moment, but at the last second, your car just as suddenly comes out of the spin and you barely miss colliding with the wall!

After completely emptying your bladder...and firing a few choice words at your instructor...he tells you to start driving again! This time you might try to keep an eye on that cursed little box, attempting to anticipate another spinout, but ultimately you have to focus all your attention on maneuvering the 2,000+ pounds of metal and engine at 130+ mph. Once again, the rise in adrenaline, the speed of the car, the roar of the engine, and the blur... and, when you least expect it, another button is hit and you find yourself in another wild, uncontrolled spinout. Each button throws you into a different spin that, against your best efforts, you cannot possibly anticipate. Once again, the instructor grabs your head and focuses your attention on where the car needs to go, and once again, at the final moment before impact, the car comes out of the spin just missing the approaching wall.

By experience, you begin to learn that your hands follow what your eyes are focused on and the car eventually aligns itself in the direction with which the wheels are facing. You then understand what the instructor is trying to teach you. The point is not to try to anticipate what button will be pressed or when the spinout might happen. That is the instructor's job. You will never figure that one out. Your responsibility is where to direct your focused attention.

Now, focus. Let's answer a couple of questions.

1. What aspect of your life is spinning out of control?
2. What direction are you supposed to be traveling in?
3. Where is your focus?

Your focus determines where, how, and if you will recover from the spinout. It does not matter how you got there as much as it does what you will do now. Your body will carry out what your mind is focused on.

God is in control. Stop trying to figure out what His next move will be and let Him do His job. He knows what He is doing.

Get focused!

Go Deeper: Philippians 4:8

Vision

"Where there is no vision, the people perish..." Proverbs 29:18

The word vision implies purpose, meaning and reason. Vision also involves direction, though the details may not be known. Where there is a vision, there is depth; and any successful corporation or business operation demonstrates that where there is no vision, no purpose, no direction...there is death. Walking out a vision shows us who we are, Whose we are, and it reveals the fact that we have a great purpose.

In John 1:42 when Andrew first brought Peter, his brother, to meet Jesus, Jesus greeted Peter by saying, "Thou art Simon the son of Jona: thou shalt be called 'Cephas,' which is by interpretation, a 'stone.'" Jesus began to lay the vision for Peter's life before him during their first meeting, and the acceptance of that vision by Peter would ultimately change his life forever. All that Peter knew of his life was what was before his eyes. He was a fisherman that worked to make ends meet, living in a country that was oppressed and overtaxed by the ancient Roman government. Jesus, on the other hand, knew a very different reality for Peter. Jesus knew that God had purposed that Peter should become one of the greatest teachers of the Gospel that the world had ever known. Peter viewed himself a fisherman; Jesus viewed him as a "fisher of men." While Peter was known to be impetuous, foul-mouthed, and rough, Jesus knew that the grace of God would change Peter into a fervently passionate servant of God who would finally stand so firmly for Christ, that to crucify him upside down would not turn him from his Master. Until Peter began to behold the vision that Jesus laid out for his life, though, he simply existed from day to day as many of us do now.

Notwithstanding Christ's vision for Peter's life, Satan also had a vision and an interpretation of who Peter was. It was Satan's plan that Peter should completely desert Christ and live a humiliated, guilty existence for the rest of his life. More than that, Jesus told Peter, "...Satan hath desired to have you, that he may sift you as wheat: but I have prayed for thee, that thy faith fail not...," Luke 22:31,32. If we do not accept the vision that Christ has for us, the enemy will always impose his reality on us. The enemy will always have his interpretation of who we are. That is why before Peter's greatest personal failure occurred, Christ encouraged Peter by affirming the vision; "When thou art converted, strengthen your brethren," Luke 22:32. After Peter's awful abandonment of Christ, he remembered and acted on the vision that the Savior had laid out. Acts 2:14-42 demonstrates that Peter accepted Christ's vision for his life.

People all over the world suffer in many ways because they are convinced that what they see is all that there is. It is the reason that we witness high percentages of high school and college dropouts. It is the reason that many leave their husbands or their wives. It is the reason that kids turn to gang violence and drugs. So many people around the world have no vision for their lives and with no answers, no direction, and no sense of purpose; they give up on life and begin considering the best way out of it.

The interesting thing about all this is that so few believe that there is a Creator and Author of life that has actually designed a grand plan for their lives. It has not occurred to them that there is a reason for each person's unique mix of talents, gifts, burdens, inner desires, and dreams. People have either never heard or do not care that God says, "I know the thoughts that I think toward you...thoughts of peace, and not evil to give you an expected end," Jeremiah 29:11. Why is it that so few of us have even asked God what His revealed vision is for our lives?

If surrendering to God's will for your life is what you desire, stop right now and incorporate these three steps:

One – Learn to worship God. Worship to God redirects our thinking. Praise to God invites communion, and God loves to pour into us His wonderful thoughts about us.

Two – Ask God to help you trust Him and His vision for you. It may happen immediately, or there may be a process. Let Him decide which it will be.

Three – Take the time to meditate on the principles and promises God has given. It is not enough to hear what God thinks of you — it must become who you are.

***Envision More:** Ephesians 5:17*

Temptation

"And the Lord said unto Satan,
'Hast thou considered my servant Job...?'" Job 1:8

After reading Job 1:6-12, I keep concluding that God put Job out on Front Street. The devil was "walking to and fro" on the Earth, doing what he does best, but when he had come before God with the "sons" of God, it was God who brought up Job's name, not Satan. Maybe Satan was thinking about Job anyway, maybe not. But, the challenge seemed to be offered from God Himself concerning Job. God said, "Hast thou considered my servant Job, that there is none like him in the earth, a perfect and an upright man, one that feareth God, and eschewed evil?" (vs. 8). Satan did not ask or comment about him, God...well, I have to say it....God was bragging on Job! He was boasting about Job to Satan!

As I said earlier, Satan is going to do his job. Satan is the tempter, the adversary, and the "accuser of the brethren." He chose to live for sin and that will always be his motivation. Why do we expect anything different from him? We speak of the attacks of Satan as if they were an abnormality, as if they are not supposed to happen. The devil will always do his job. That's one thing you can always count on in any situation.

So if our Father uses Satan's role to ultimately strengthen our faith, doesn't that suggest how firmly God holds Satan's choke chain? That should encourage us with the reality that Satan truly cannot step over the boundaries that God has set for him. Look at the dynamics and tell me who, really, is in control.

No matter what direction the devil has come from to try to attack you, it has to have been sized-up, measured off, shaved down, and approved by God before it can get to you. If it has gotten to you, you can know by the very nature of God that it is here because it is meant for your empowerment in some area. God never allows trials to wipe you out with no hope of recovery. What this means is that whatever you are facing or will face, no matter how difficult it may seem it can be surmounted. I Corinthians 10: 13 says, "There hath no temptation taken you but such as is common to man: but God is faithful, who will not suffer you to be tempted above that ye are able; but will with the temptation also make a way to escape, that you may be able to bear it."

Called and Chosen

"For many are called, but few are chosen." Matthew 22:14

What makes the difference in those that are called and those that are chosen? Is everybody called, or are there only a few that have the privilege of being called by God? In December of 1990, my brother, Mark, informed me that Mervyn Warren was leaving the group and that I was being considered by Take 6 to replace him. Mark suggested, and I agreed, that I should give prayerful consideration to the invitation. In my joy, I ran to tell my friends that I was being considered!

In Matthew 22:1-14, Jesus tells a parable to His listeners about a wedding celebration. A certain king invites many to the great celebration of his son's wedding. Great preparation was made in anticipation of the favored guests, but, surprisingly, some took the invitation lightly, and others flatly refused. In addition, the servants bearing the news were treated horribly and slain for announcing the invitation. In anger for the treatment of his innocent servants, the king destroyed the city and the murderers in it but announced to his remaining servants that there was still a celebration to be had for his son. Therefore, the invitation was sent out to guests to whom the invitation had not been originally given, but who might love to come. At the end of the parable, the statement is made by Jesus that "many are called, but few are chosen."

Truly, the invitation to join Take 6 was unbelievable! Many were so much more talented and could easily fill the position. I questioned why I was on the list at all. But what if I'd taken it a step further? What if the news was so inconceivable, so mind-blowing, so hard to believe, that I decided that I wouldn't believe it at all. I mean, there were so many singers that could read music with smoother voices and greater ranges. What if I decided that I wouldn't accept the invite until I'd learned to read music, and increased my vocal range? As it stood, Take 6 was prepared to train me in all areas that I was deficient. In fact, the training I needed was included in the process of inviting me to join the group. But what if I simply didn't believe it was for me?

    Interestingly enough, John 15:16 tells us that we didn't choose Christ, but that He chose us. 1 Peter 2:9 says that we are "a chosen generation, a royal priesthood," and a "holy nation..." Ephesians 1:4 says that we'd been chosen in Christ since "before the foundation of the world, that we should be holy and without blame before Him in love." Becoming holy and being blameless is already part of the process. It's included in the invitation and it isn't even our responsibility. Making us holy is the job of the One Who has chosen and called us! Just like the king in the parable, even the wedding garments have already been provided. The sole circumstance that can derail this all around "Win-Win" situation is that I refuse to believe it! The only factor that could truly have wrecked me joining Take 6 would have been that I didn't believe it, thus refusing membership. Could it be that many are called, and few are chosen because few believe? I believed, and I joined Take 6. If I believe God's invitation is for me, I'll join God's great dinner party. I've been called, and I've been chosen...as have you! The vital question now is, do you believe it?"

Go Deeper: Matthew 22:1-14, 1 Peter 2:9

Consider

"To God, who is able to do immeasurably far beyond what we can ask or think, and who wants to do even more for us by His power in our lives...," Ephesians 3:20

December 15, 2003: I was debating about whether to try to post a devotional thought every month. I did not know if I could commit to the responsibility. I continually weighed the doubts with the positives, and I kept coming up more doubtful than positive. I finally decided to post the first devotional thought in spite of my unanswered questions. This time last year I had a research paper due for school that I had given up on. I was in a program working toward my undergraduate degree that should have only taken 18 months to finish. I had made it a six-year program. I was discouraged by my lack of action. The paper seemed impossible to finish, especially since my computer had crashed, and since I would need to be re-introduced to my advisor, figuring that he had surely forgotten who I was by now.

Last year this time, I was invited to go speak in London and South Africa, but I had never been out of the country without Take 6, and I could not see how it could be done. I had always been bound to my special comfort zone, and I was afraid to leave it to grow, even as a speaker. I debated the idea of simply not answering the request and letting the invitation dissolve. I could not fail at something I did not attempt, right? If you asked me about having children this time last year, I would have artfully avoided your question. I could not see being responsible for someone else, that could not begin to give back to me.

This time last year, I was convinced I should have been out of debt, but I had somehow missed my opportunity and my financial scene would remain unchanged for the rest of my life. I could not sell my car because I owed too much on it, but I could not seem to keep myself from being two months behind every month. Last year I had personal demons I had never been able to overcome, and it looked as though they were not going anywhere. That was last year.

December 15 2004: Because of all the inner victories God has helped me get, outer victories simply follow suit. I received the title to my car from the bank as I finished the last payment, which has tremendously freed me up financially, and has moved me closer to being out of debt. Three months have passed since I've visited London and South Africa. I have new brothers and sisters in these countries, and I was given the new name "Sephiwe" which is a Zulu name meaning "special gift." The experience changed my life forever and I cannot imagine not having taken the risk of moving out of my comfort zone. Upon my departure from South Africa, I was given the gift of an infant sweater for an infant I didn't presently have. Now I have a beautiful baby girl! I finished that "impossible" research paper at the end of last April. When I actually applied myself to it, it had only taken a couple of weeks to revive and complete. I had made it larger than it really was.

I don't know what will be accomplished by December 15, 2005. So many impossible events became possible this year, so many personal demons have been defeated, so many life battles have been won in the period of one year, so many people have been healed through prayer...what might be the possibilities this time next year? God is absolutely amazing! The only resolution I have for 2005 is the same one I made last year: "By the grace of God, I simply commit not to work against God once He sets His plans in motion." His plans are so great; I am the one who has kept Him from being more successful in my life. Not again. I think you might want to at least check back with me this time next year. God has truly exceeded my expectations! So, how will your life look this time next year?

Go Deeper: *Share the blessings of the last year with at least one other person that God leads you to before this year ends.*

Victory

*"Every place that the sole of your foot
will tread upon I have given you..." Joshua 1:3*

Moses was dead. Joshua was now the leader in the camp of Israel. God used Moses to lead the children out of Egypt, through the desert, to the border of the Promised Land. Joshua was to lead Israel into the land that God had promised to give them as an inheritance. There was one major problem, though — there were people still living on the land. The heathen Canaanites were not about to give up their possession to a bunch of deluded ex-slaves. The Canaanites were stubborn, violent, and large.

What happens when you are confronted with the promise and the threat? In fact, it is fair to conclude that where there is a promise, there will always be a threat. Since you cannot accommodate both, you must choose which one you will believe and submit to. Either you will take authority over your addiction, or it will take authority over you. You will overcome that debilitating fear, or it will overcome you. You will break free of your bondage or you and everyone who depends on you will remain hopeless slaves, forever. There is no middle ground.

Here is your promise: God has given you the land. You must take possession of it. He has promised to put the muscle behind your decision, but you must decide. "Every place that the sole of your foot will tread upon, I have given you..." Everywhere that you must walk this year, God has given you. Every situation that you find yourself confronted with, seen or unseen, God has given you. The land is yours, but you must believe it and then take authority.

Now, where is your foot? What are you standing on right now? Is your marriage hanging by a thread? Is your job security dangling? Are you struggling to pass a class? Do you feel alone? Are you suffering with depression? Have they put the pink notice on your desk, the door of your house, or the clipboard of your hospital bed? Are you about to be promoted? Will your promotion bring more responsibility? Are you going into new territory? Where is your foot? God's promise is that whatever the circumstance, whatever the challenge, whatever valley must be passed through, He has given you that territory as a victory and an inheritance. That means that what you gain as a victory out of all this, God will give you to pass on to someone else. It is yours.

"No man shall be able to stand before you all the days of your life; as I was with Moses, so I will be with you. I will not leave you nor forsake you," Joshua 1:5. "Only be strong and very courageous, that you may observe to do according to all the law which Moses My servant commanded you; do not turn from it to the right hand or to the left, that you may prosper wherever you go," Joshua 1:7.

Additional Reading: Joshua 1:1-9

To Shine by Night

"Thus says the Lord, Who gives the sun for a light by day, the ordinances of the moon and the stars for a light by night..."
Jeremiah 31:35

The other evening, I walked out onto my balcony into the cold of night. I looked up into the crystal-clear sky and took in the beautiful scene. The stars glittered like diamonds against the backdrop of space, and there in the midst of the sky was the brightest object — the moon.

While I gazed, I began to realize that this celestial nightlight has often been credited with lighting up the darkness of the evening. In all truth, the moon emits no light of its own. It does not have the power or the resource to generate that type of energy. Quite simply, the moon is a mass of craters and rock covered with dust. Man has touched down on the moon and kicked up the dust that covers the whole landscape. The light we attribute to the moon actually comes from the sun. The sun is that celestial body of solar energy that is responsible for radiating light and heat. There is nothing about the moon that is worthy of any glory.

One of the primary purposes of the moon is its ability to reflect. The light of the moon that is visible to us is directly proportionate to how much of it is exposed to the sun. If the moon is directly exposed to the sun's light, it shines fully and brightly. If something cuts off any part of that light, only part of the moon is visible. You can witness the effects of this principle during a lunar eclipse. The Earth moves into the path between the sun and the moon, the sun's light is interrupted, and the moon has nothing to reflect. Without exposure to the sun, the moon loses one of its primary functions.

It began to dawn on me that one of our best qualities as humans is our ability to reflect. There is no glory in anything we are or feel we are able to do. The Bible says that all of our righteousness is equivalent to a stack of soiled rags (Isaiah 64:6). The best we feel we can offer is about as worthless as the dust on the moon's surface. Most importantly, the extent of our effectiveness on this earth is proportionate to our exposure to the character of God in our lives. The more of God's light we expose ourselves to, the brighter our lives shine in this dark world. Consequently, when we allow some body, some object or some circumstance to eclipse the divine light that shines on us, our true purpose is veiled in the resulting darkness. As long as the Light is interrupted, our purpose remains in the shadows. In fact, when we are fully exposed to God, His glory illuminates our experiences so brightly, that people can mistakenly attribute His light to us.

It is the job of the Son of God to shine. It is our job to reflect His light. When we do what we are called to do, we transfer the greatest glory to the darkest of situations. The moon does its best job at night. It was created for dark situations. You and I were created to shine in dark situations. We were created to reflect that light in whatever circumstance we find ourselves. So, understand that the circumstance itself doesn't matter so much as what we are to be in that circumstance...a light; but, your responsibility is not even to generate light. You cannot. That is not in your nature. That is God's responsibility. All you need is full exposure, so you can reflect.

Go Deeper: Isaiah 60:19, II Corinthians 4:3-6

It Needs More Salt!

"Ye are the salt of the earth . . . Ye are the light of the world..."
Matthew 5:13, 14

I came to understand the meaning of these verses when Take 6 was asked to perform as part of a huge tribute to a pop star a couple of years ago. Generally, I did not have a problem performing in any venue that Take 6 was called to because we normally performed music from our own repertoire. On this Friday night, though, we were asked to perform one of the artist's songs. I was particularly uncomfortable, but after voicing my opinion, I dropped the issue for the sake of time.

Interestingly enough, as we were waiting to perform later on in the evening, I found myself again questioning why we were not singing our own material. I asked myself, "What glory could God get here if I'm not singing some song or saying something about Him?" Having been raised in a conservative religion, I was having a difficult time justifying my presence at the tribute concert of a pop star. Sounds silly?

Now, do not be confused. I firmly believe that as a follower of Christ, my steps are ordered by God (Psalm 37:23). This means that sometimes I will find myself in the most unexpected places for lifting up the name of Christ. Take 6 has performed many times in venues that are considered "questionable" by the church people; but like Christ, we are sent to "seek and to save that which was lost," Luke 19:10. And many people who need to hear about God's love will not step foot in a church. On the other hand, I have finished doing concerts at clubs and have been moved by the Spirit to leave immediately. My only responsibility has been to obey.

This was one of those instances that found me wondering what God was up to.

I was speaking to Cedric about it the next day when he shared something very interesting with me. In essence, there are times when God wants me to be a "light" to a darkened world as Matthew 5:14 states. In the Bible, light is often synonymous with the knowledge of God as stated in John 12:36, or Acts 26:18. I am more familiar with these instances of being a light because usually I am verbally singing or talking about His love to people. Light is shining upon a situation (Matthew 5:16).

What I did not think about was Matthew 5:13. There are times when God uses me in the context of salt. Have you ever thought about the properties of salt? Salt is mixed into a situation and has a profound influence on its environment. Think about it...have you ever heard someone refer to a tasty, well-seasoned lasagna, and comment, "Now that was excellent salt!" Maybe you have heard someone say, "The cookies were delicious, but the salt that was used to make them was outstanding!"

Salt, added in just the right proportion, makes the dish taste great, but the focus is not the salt itself. The focus is on the great tasting dish. If the salt ever becomes the focus, you can bet that you have either added too much, or you have not added enough; yet, the influence of the salt is definitely discerned. In short, salt can make an otherwise tasteless situation wonderful.

The more we walk with God, the more "seasoned" we become. Intimacy with God gives our lives the "savor" spoken of in Matthew 5:13, or the "saltiness" that Mark 9:50 talks about. As a result, God allows us to be sprinkled into situations that would be otherwise tasteless, or distasteful, so that He can get the glory. God may need to mix me into a crowded subway, a grid-locked traffic jam, or a family reunion. He might sprinkle me into a beautiful wedding ceremony, or a darkened hospital room, just so He can season the atmosphere with His presence. Maybe God has been in a transaction you were making at a bank that was scheduled to be robbed, but the plans were not able to be carried out. Maybe you were a victim in a flood shelter where your faith kept someone beside you from giving up. What if God wants to be revealed through you as a patient of cancer, or as a child in a single-parent family? Who knows what joy or hope was brought to someone around you because your presence was salt to a tasteless condition?

Maybe the point is not so much what the circumstance is, but how Christ can be demonstrated through it. Maybe it just needs more salt...somebody like you.

Go Deeper: II Corinthians 4:10, Mark 9:5

Truth

"Now, therefore, behold, the cry of the children of Israel is come unto Me: and I have also seen the oppression wherewith the Egyptians oppress them." Exodus 3:9

Oppression is the forcing of someone else's reality on me. According to the Hebrew word for oppress which is "Yanah," to be oppressed is the state of being vexed, mistreated, done wrong, overreached, and driven away. The children of Israel were "oppressed" by the Egyptians. According to the Egyptians, Israel's reality was to be perpetual slaves. They were thought of as less than human — not worthy of the right to life. They were vexed, mistreated, done wrong, overreached, and driven away.

Many times, the enemy oppresses me. He loves to vex me with his reality and his interpretation of my circumstances. Especially when I do not know what God is doing in my life or how He is working, the devil jumps at the opportunity to give me his take on what God is or is not doing for me. His thoughts are oppressing. If you let him, the enemy will sympathize with you, fill you with self-pity, and then suggest a way out of the madness. Do not be surprised...his way out is generally death. More specifically, it is you taking your own life.

You know, I am not really even upset with the devil anymore when he comes to oppress. That is his rightful job as "accuser of the brethren." He is the father of lies, and he will always mix a little truth with a little error to accomplish his purposes. It is his reality that is dark, hopeless, and full of defeat, not mine. But, understand, the moment I believe what he says about me, oppression then becomes depression. Now his thoughts are in me because I have accepted them as the truth. This is what he wants. He can remain around me to oppress, or he can leave me, but I will recycle the belief in his reality that I have chosen within my own heart.

Now, let me give you three mighty weapons that you can use against oppression and depression. The first of these weapons is worship. Learn to worship God. Do not wait until you feel like it, or until you can see your way out. Decide to worship God in the middle of your ordeal. Lift Him up. Tell Him how good He is. Find a Psalm and make it your own. Find a song of worship and turn it up. When Job was tried and everything was taken away, Job fell down without any apparent reason and worshiped God (Job 1:20). Worship takes all focus off you and places it directly on our Father. Worship aligns our lives with the Creator, resets our priorities, and prepares us to receive the next weapon.

The next mighty weapon that I will share with you is described as the "belt" of the whole armor of God mentioned in Ephesians 6:10-18. Look it up. Do you see it? The weapon is truth. Let me show you why this is a weapon. The word "truth" in the New Testament comes from a Greek word "Aletheia." This word defines truth as the "unveiled reality lying at the basis of and agreeing with an appearance . . . the reality clearly lying before our eyes as opposite a mere appearance, without reality."

The truth exposes all types of lies. God describes His Spirit as the Spirit of truth. Whether I am oppressed or depressed, I have learned to ask myself two questions. The first question is, "What does God say about this situation?" The second is, "What has God promised me concerning this situation?" Whatever the circumstance, you must answer these questions for yourself according to the Word of God. The enemy of our souls will always give you the "mere appearance, without reality." The enemy cannot contend with God or His Word. When God is near, you will always have the unveiled reality, because God is truth (John 14:6, 16:13). As light exposes darkness, the Truth will always expose the lie. When I believe that He is the unveiled reality, and that His promises are for me, His promises set me free from the enemy's lies (John 8:32). Ask God to reveal the truth about your situation.

The third weapon is, in fact, God's promises. Jesus said that man does not live by bread alone, but by every word that proceeds out of the mouth of God (Luke 4:4). The devil could not contend with Jesus, and he cannot contend with Jesus in you when you live and breathe God's promises. Look again to Ephesians 6:10-18, and see what the sword of the Spirit is. What is it? It is God's Word. Why is God's Word described as a sword? Hebrews 4:12, 13 says that the Word of God is quick and powerful and sharper than any two-edged sword. The Word of God cuts up the enemy and his lies, and God's promises reveal the truth.

I have found that the practice of worshiping God pulls the rug out from under the enemy's oppression and frees me from depression. Asking God for the truth about my situation exposes the mere appearance of reality proposed by the enemy, and gives me a peace in knowing that what God sees is the unveiled reality. Finally, believing God's promises to me puts the final nail in the devil's sophistry. If my Father has promised me life, regardless of what the devil makes me feel, I will have life, and life more abundantly. Are you oppressed? Are you depressed? What has God said about your situation? What has God promised you concerning your situation?

> **Go Deeper:** *"And ye shall know the truth, and the truth shall set you free," John 8:32*

Diamond

"For since the creation of the world God's invisible qualities – his eternal power and divine nature – have been clearly seen, being understood from what has been made, so that men are without excuse." Romans 1:20

Where do diamonds come from? How are they made? Diamonds start out as ordinary, common carbon; but the difference in the ordinary carbon and the extraordinary diamond is the process.

First, the diamond-forming process takes you into the bowels of the earth...very deep. Diamonds are forged deep inside the earth's crust, approximately 75 to 150 miles down into the earth. Above 75 miles' depth, the other elements of the process can't even be activated.

The next ingredient in the process of diamond creation is heat and it must be intense. The closer one comes to the core of the earth the hotter the temperature. The center of the earth is estimated to burn at around 12,000 degrees Fahrenheit. So, only at such depths as 100+ miles below can the elements begin to establish heat between 1600 and 2300 degrees Fahrenheit. At this heat, rock and other elements are effectively melted down, altering the carbon.

Within these depths, the next ingredient of the process can be introduced...pressure. Pressure can better be expressed in gigapaschals. For diamonds to form, they've got to have an incredible amount of pressure, so at least five gigapascals of pressure are necessary. 5 gigapaschals of pressure are equal to about 104,427,171 pounds of pressure per square foot, or 725,188 pounds of pressure per square inch!

Now, along with the last element, time, the right ingredients are in place to produce a valuable substance. Only long periods of time, coupled with intense heat and tremendous pressure at great depths can transform common carbon by drastically acting upon its element until carbon crystallizes. At just the right time, the constant action forces the crystallized carbon in melted rock upward within lava channels that transport the rock containing the crystallized carbon toward the surface, where the brutalized element can cool to a degree. Any longer under such pressures and the common carbon would simply disintegrate.

The same wonderful Creator whose natural factory creates value in common carbon also creates valuable jewels from common men and women, and the process isn't much different. I will be continually amazed at how God leads His servants into great depths of circumstance, only to be melted by intense heat, strained under great pressure over tough lengths of time, until their very character, hidden in Christ, crystallizes in Him. At some times, it seems that the process will completely consume the jewels of His desire, but just as the crystalline carbon is transported upward in enough time to allow it to cool and not be consumed, so God takes His jewels out of the furnace at the right time, and not a second too soon, or too late, for His attention to detail is diligent and specific. He will not allow us to "be tempted beyond what we can bear." -1 Cor. 10:13 (NIV)

The world has attempted to break the follower of Christ in every way, but like the diamond, the Truth embedded in the character of the follower of Christ cuts deep into the unstable and shifting ways of the world. The very word "diamond" comes from a Greek word "adamas" that literally means "unbreakable." And one day, the fiery glory of the Most High God will shine through the lives of His human diamonds, and they will glitter, and sparkle in the light of His presence before the inhabitants of the earth. Everyone will then understand as never before, as they gaze upon the saved, transformed men and women who were as ordinary and as common as carbon, that the difference in the ordinary and the extraordinary, is the process.

Don't Become Weary

*"And let us not be weary in well doing:
for in due season we shall reap, if we faint not."* Gal. 6:9

I know everyone has felt like throwing in the towel at some point. Someone's felt like walking away from the job or if you're really honest, someone's felt like walking away from that marriage that just seems too hard to deal with. I know the feeling when all you've invested seems lost and you just feel like "fainting."

I was practicing "sprint training" on the treadmill a few years ago. My trainer had me doing sprints this way: the treadmill would be turned up to 9 or 10 miles an hour and from a stance of straddling the sides of the treadmill in resting position, I would have to jump on and sprint or run for one minute straight. When that minute was finished, I would jump off and rest for only 30 seconds before I would have to start the next one-minute sprint. This exercise would continue until I had done a total of 10 one-minute sprints.

While this entire exercise took a total of 15 minutes, after the second of ten sprints, my lungs burned like fire, and 30 seconds seemed inadequate to even stand up straight before starting the next sprint, much less catching my breath. Running full speed made a short minute feel like an hour! My focus had to be trained to such an extent that I would only look forward, keeping my head as straight as possible. Any action that was not congruent with close-to-perfect form would detract from my focus and threaten to launch me backward from the treadmill. During my 30-second rest, I didn't have the spare breath to so much as complain to my trainer. Every precious second was spent trying to gain as much oxygen as possible, for the next sprint was coming very quickly.

It goes without saying that anywhere between sprint number two and sprint number 10, I was in constant contemplation of quitting both the exercise and the workout completely. When an untrained body is under high stress, the only thought is to rid itself of such strenuous conditions. If such conditions are engaged by choice, it only seems natural that by choice, one can just as easily quit.

I would say that since 1991, when I joined Take 6, I've noticed that any one of the six of us have become so weary with the group that we would have been willing to quit at least once. As a group, we have simply learned to give that individual space to deal with his feelings and evaluate the circumstances. The truth is that, very often, finances can be strained, interpersonal relationships can be strained, and external family situations can put enough pressure on the individual so that it seems easier to simply leave the group. In the end, we have all realized that we have been called to this organization by God, and until His purpose is finished, it would behoove us to remain steadfast and not give up.

I believe that Paul felt this type of weariness at times when his mind and heart began to ache for relief from "running the race." One can simply get to the place where he or she feels like everything he or she has invested: time, money, patience, means, and even the will to continue on, like wasted seed, has been spent in vain. One can feel as though there will either be no harvest and no return on investment, or that the perceived return isn't sufficient to justify the immense output of energy to keep going.

But the Word of the Lord says in Galatians 6:9, "...in due season we *shall reap*, if we faint not." The Lord of the harvest, Who created and established the law of sowing and reaping has promised that as we continue to labor, we will surely reap what has been sown if we abide by the conditions set forth.

The first condition is hidden in the phrase, "in due season." Has the appropriate season come yet for reaping? I remember adding watermelon seeds to my garden while planting a couple of years ago. I couldn't conceal my pride as the flowering blossoms gave way to the first developing melons. Now, watermelons generally need about 70 to 90 days to mature, and I wasn't anywhere close to that time frame when I was ready to pluck the fruit. No matter how beautifully the melons were developing, the time wasn't yet right for harvesting. But in "due season," 70 to 90 days to be exact, I could look forward to ripe fruit. The season for harvest was on its way!

The other condition is "if we faint not." When God created the concept of seasons and set them in motion after the Flood, He said "While the earth remaineth, *seedtime and harvest*, and cold and heat, and summer and winter and day and night *shall not cease.*" Gen. 8:22 This statement implies that seasons are cyclical and will be so until He returns. The appropriate season for harvest is surely coming, because the change of seasons is a constant. But an individual can choose to "faint" or give up. An individual can give up on a crop just before the time of harvest moves in and lose the long awaited yield. Galatians 6:9 implies that fainting is a choice. The verse implies that God will supply strength to continue, if we don't choose to give up and quit.

Have you invested and faithfully sown? Does it seem that the season for harvest is long in coming? Do you find yourself wanting to give up the race, desiring to acquiesce to quitting? Don't give up; "for in due season we shall reap, if we faint not."

Answering with Faith

"So Moses brought Israel from the Red sea, and they went out into the wilderness of Shur; and they went three days in the wilderness, and found no water." Exodus 15:22

The children of Israel had just seen the culmination of the plagues on Egypt fulfilled when Pharaoh's army finally drowned in the sea. Since birth, all that many of the people knew was the hard bondage they were exposed to as slaves in Egypt. Four hundred years of slavery gave way to a couple of weeks of watching their tormentor, Pharaoh, be dismally dismantled before God, and in a moment, their dreaded oppressor was removed — buried in the Red Sea.

The songs had been sung and the praises were lifted to God for His mighty deliverance. Now, on their way to the Promised Land, the children of Israel traveled into the desert with high expectations. One million plus individuals, still elated about the previous days' events, headed into a dry wilderness on foot with their children and their flocks. Somewhere between the burning desert sands and the scorching sun, the children of Israel soon recognized that they were in deep need of a basic element...water. What were they thinking? Even if they could find a miracle body of water in a desert, would it be enough for over a million individuals and scores of animals? What about their children? Had not God thought about what they would need? Not more than three days had passed and already death circled above their heads — waiting for the right moment to descend upon them.

Miraculously, the multitude did stumble upon a body of water; but they were to be horridly disappointed. This area they named Marah, which meant "bitterness," and bitter it was, for the water was totally undrinkable. It seemed as though the body of water was a cruel divine joke played upon a helpless multitude. That body of water seemed to represent the entire environment: the surroundings, the circumstances, and the general attitude...bitter!

Dehydrated minds do not contemplate very well. What was God thinking? Who was Moses, really, and did he really know what he was doing? With death just lurking around the next mountain, what did it matter that God had performed such a miraculous feat of deliverance? What Pharaoh could not do to them with all his threats, the wilderness would. If they could just get to the front of the line where Moses was, they would surely give him a piece of their minds.

It is funny how the most miraculous victories can evaporate in the face of the next trial. What God accomplished in physically parting the water of the Red Sea was grand, but that was yesterday, wasn't it? We still have today to live through, with its own trials, and today's trials seem to have no respect for yesterday's victories.

Our places of bitterness set the stage for one of the most important lessons we will have to learn — dependence on God happens daily. God well knew that the next stop would be a place of extreme bitterness. Had the Israelites known this fact at the Red Sea they might have simply turned themselves over to Pharaoh without a struggle. The next lesson after the Red Sea needed to be one of dependence, for they would need God every step of the way.

It is important to understand that God was not looking for answers from the Israelites. He was not looking for them to fix the situation that they were in. He did not expect them to know how to avoid the trial. What He was looking for was faith! God Himself designed the trial and mapped out the path through the place of bitterness. He was only looking for the Israelites to answer with faith.

You do not have to know how to fix your place of

bitterness. You do not have to worry about how you could have avoided coming there. All God is calling you to do is to answer each challenge with faith in Him. "And He [Moses] cried unto the Lord; and the Lord shewed him a tree, which when he had cast into the waters, the waters were made sweet," Exodus 15:25. The Lord knows how to bring you out, and it can happen as instantly as He wants it to, using the most unusual circumstances to make it sweet. Do you think that the tree was made of sugar? No. It was not the tree. It was faith that cut down the tree and cast it into the bitter water — believing that God was all in all. That is what was sweet!

About the Author

JOEL KIBBLE is a devoted husband, father, writer, speaker, producer and member of the multi award-winning recording artists Take 6. He conveys his world-wide travels and experiences in riveting, inspiring anecdotes and pearls of wisdom. Joel's life journey forced him, through faith, to see desert passages transformed into springs of experience. Continuing his own personal transformation, Joel is dedicated to challenging others to discover living streams of water in their own dry, desert places.

Invite Joel Kibble to your church or organization.

For resources or engagements, visit:
www.joelkibble.com

VITA-Minutes: Keeping your spirit healthy.
Look for Vita-minutes at www.joelkibble.com

www.ingramcontent.com/pod-product-compliance
Lightning Source LLC
Chambersburg PA
CBHW050600300426
44112CB00013B/2010